"This book is rich with clinical dialogues that help readers put into practice the collaborative, transtheoretical ideas and methods of strengths-based therapy. SBT challenges the assumptions of diagnosis-based treatments and offers an alternative client-directed approach. A must read for mental health practitioners and graduate students."

Michael J. Lambert, Ph.D., Professor, Brigham Young University. Editor of *Bergin and Garfield's Handbook of Psychotherapy and Behavior Change*

"Whether you're a novice and simply curious about Strength-Based Therapy, or an experienced SBT clinician, this book is a must read. It offers an in-depth understanding of the roots of this client-centered therapy approach, a clear description of its components along with clinical examples that bring the ideas to life. Regardless of your current theoretical model, if you want better outcomes with your clients—and more enjoyment from your work—you will greatly benefit from this practical guide."

Michele Weiner-Davis, LCSW.
Co-author of *In Search of Solutions: A New Direction in Psychotherapy*

"I am very excited to see the publication of this book. Emphasizing a strength-based approach to therapy is not only a needed addition to current practice, it is a needed corrective. Fostering strength is one of the best ways to correct psychopathology. The book provides an excellent theoretical and research base for this approach, and follows it up with a whole set of useful suggestions for strength-based practice."

Arthur C. Bohart, Professor Emeritus, California State University-Dominguez Hills. Author of *How Clients Make Therapy Work: The Process of Active Self-Healing*

"It is clear from the research that clients—not therapists—are the principal driving force behind positive therapeutic change. This unique and compelling book shows how counsellors and psychotherapists can capitalise on that and help clients make the most of their therapy. Accessible, informed and illustrated throughout with client studies and dialogues, *Strengths-Based Therapy* can help therapists of all orientations develop their practice in a client-centred, outcome-informed, and socially-just direction. An invaluable addition to the contemporary counselling and psychotherapy literature."

Mick Cooper, Professor, University of Roehampton.
Co-author of *Pluralistic Counselling and Psychotherapy*

"Read *Strength-Based Therapy* and improve your therapeutic success rate. Murphy and Sparks share a thought-provoking non-pathologizing therapy in which client wisdom is championed as a major ingredient of successful outcome. They generously illustrate this with their wealth of clinical experience—showing their embodiment of respect and humility, and importantly, exemplifying 'doing social justice.'"

Harlene Anderson, Ph.D., International Consultant,
The Toas Institute, Houston Galveston Institute

Strengths-Based Therapy

Strengths-Based Therapy: Distinctive Features offers an introduction to what is distinctive about this innovative client-directed approach. Written by two experienced practitioners of strengths-based therapies, this book translates SBT principles and practices into concise, evidence-based ideas and techniques that mental health practitioners can immediately apply on the job. Using the popular Distinctive Features format, this book describes 15 theoretical features and 15 practical techniques of Strengths-Based Therapy.

Strengths-Based Therapy will be a valuable resource for psychotherapists, clinical, health and counseling psychologists, counselors, psychiatrists, marriage and family therapists, social workers, and all who wish to know more about this unique approach to therapy.

John J. Murphy, Professor of Psychology at the University of Central Arkansas (USA), is an internationally recognized clinician and trainer of client-directed, strengths-based therapies. His books have been translated into multiple languages and he has trained thousands of helping professionals throughout the world.

Jacqueline A. Sparks is a Professor of Couple and Family Therapy in the College of Health Sciences at the University of Rhode Island (USA). She has written and trained extensively on the use of systematic client feedback in psychotherapy to promote client voice and choice.

Psychotherapy and Counselling Distinctive Features
Series Editor: Windy Dryden

The Psychotherapy and Counselling Distinctive Features series provides readers with an introduction to the distinctive theoretical and practical features of various therapeutic approaches from leading practitioners in their field.

Each book in this series focuses on one particular approach and guides the reader through 30 features—both theoretical and practical—that are particularly distinctive of that approach. Written for practitioners by practitioners, this series will also be of interest to trainees, social workers, and many others outside the therapeutic tradition.

Titles in the series:

Pluralistic Therapy by John McLeod

Cognitive Analytic Therapy by Claire Corbridge, Laura Brummer and Philippa Coid

Existential Therapy by Emmy van Deurzen and Claire Arnold-Baker

Strengths-Based Therapy by John Murphy and Jacqueline Sparks

For further information about this series please visit:

www.routledge.com/Psychotherapy-and-Counselling-Distinctive-Features/book-series/PCDF

Strengths-Based Therapy

Distinctive Features

John J. Murphy and Jacqueline A. Sparks

LONDON AND NEW YORK

First published 2018
by Routledge
2 Park Square, Milton Park, Abingdon, Oxon OX14 4RN

and by Routledge
711 Third Avenue, New York, NY 10017

Routledge is an imprint of the Taylor & Francis Group, an informa business

© 2018 John J. Murphy and Jacqueline A. Sparks

The right of John J. Murphy and Jacqueline A. Sparks to be identified as the authors of this work has been asserted by them in accordance with sections 77 and 78 of the Copyright, Designs and Patents Act 1988.

All rights reserved. No part of this book may be reprinted or reproduced or utilised in any form or by any electronic, mechanical, or other means, now known or hereafter invented, including photocopying and recording, or in any information storage or retrieval system, without permission in writing from the publishers.

Trademark notice: Product or corporate names may be trademarks or registered trademarks, and are used only for identification and explanation without intent to infringe.

British Library Cataloguing-in-Publication Data
A catalogue record for this book is available from the British Library

Library of Congress Cataloging-in-Publication Data
A catalog record for this book has been requested

ISBN: 978-1-138-68410-2 (hbk)
ISBN: 978-1-138-68414-0 (pbk)
ISBN: 978-1-315-51297-6 (ebk)

Typeset in Times New Roman and Frutiger
by Florence Production Ltd, Stoodleigh, Devon, UK

Contents

List of figures	ix
Foreword	xi
Preface	xv
Acknowledgments	xvii
Abbreviations	xix

Part 1 DISTINCTIVE THEORETICAL FEATURES OF SBT — 1

1. History of SBT — 3
2. SBT as transtheoretical and value added — 9
3. Clients as heroes of change — 13
4. SBT as client directed — 17
5. SBT and therapist factors — 21
6. SBT and the therapeutic alliance — 25
7. SBT and hope — 29
8. SBT and social constructionism — 33
9. SBT language and practices — 37
10. SBT and diagnosis — 41
11. SBT as systemic — 45
12. Cultural considerations in SBT — 49
13. Social justice and SBT — 53
14. SBT and client feedback — 57
15. Challenges of SBT practice — 61

Part 2 DISTINCTIVE PRACTICAL FEATURES OF SBT 65

16 Being respectfully curious   67
17 Validating clients   71
18 Instilling hope   75
19 Exploring clients' theories of change   81
20 Exploring clients' desired future   85
21 Recruiting client resources   91
22 Listening for change   97
23 Asking resilience and coping questions   101
24 Building on exceptions   105
25 Co-creating new stories   111
26 Using between-session strategies   117
27 Collecting systematic client feedback   121
28 Creating strengths-based work environments   127
29 Integrating SBT into training and supervision 133
30 Acting for social justice   141

Appendix A   145
References   151
Index   161

Figures

21.1	Example of completed Outcome Rating Scale (ORS) using Better Outcomes Now (BON) in couple therapy	95
27.1	Better Outcomes Now (BON) graph with client's ORS scores (thick bottom line) and expected treatment response (ETR) (long middle line). Progress meter shows client to be less than 50% of ETR, suggesting a client/counselor conversation about changing therapeutic directions	123
28.1	Example of SBT Site Assessment Grid	128
29.1	Better Outcomes Now (BON) rater page depicting at-risk clients (i.e., clients with arrows to the left)	137
29.2	Better Outcomes Now (BON) graph displaying client's ORS scores (bottom line), ETR (middle line), and SRS scores (top line)	138

Foreword

There is no one on the planet for whom I'd rather write a foreword than these authors and there's no book that I'd rather have people read in the mental health and substance abuse fields than this one. High praise indeed. Let me tell you why. First, the authors: John J. Murphy and Jacqueline A. Sparks exemplify everything that's right about providing services to clients and embody the original aspirations of why many of us got into this profession in the first place—to make a meaningful difference in the lives of those we serve. Drs. Murphy and Sparks have done everything they encourage you to do in this book. Interestingly, both started on the front lines collaborating with heroic clients to overcome adversity in all the varied ways it presents itself to human experience. There is no one I'd rather have on my team, behind the mirror, or in the room with me while I see clients. I have first-hand experience of their work and it has always served as an inspiration of what our field can be. And they have been writing about and teaching these ideas for many years to students and practitioners worldwide. This book brings a wealth of experience to the table from two extremely gifted practitioners, teachers, and scholars.

There is something else that needs to be said about the authors. Strengths-based therapy (SBT) has been derided over the years as naïve as well as many other derogatory descriptions. Sadly, the prevailing perspective to view those we serve as broken, scarred, incomplete, or sick provides fierce resistance to an alternative that privileges client ideas and resources throughout the therapeutic process. But certain individuals held strong and did not succumb (to the dark side of the Force) to view clients in terms of the "Killer Ds:" diagnosis, disorder, deficit, dysfunction, or damaged. Jacqueline Sparks and John Murphy fought the battles in both practice and print year after year to view clients well beyond and far greater than the pathological labels we bestow upon them. Your authors were undaunted by the dominant discourse of pathology and have been on the right side of this ongoing values argument long before it was fashionable.

And now this book: Drs. Murphy and Sparks combine this treasure trove of experiences—clinical, teaching, and standing up to practices that diminish clients—with a conceptual tour de force that takes strengths-based therapy to a new level. They identify the roots of SBT, pay appropriate homage to key players, cogently describe its theoretical underpinnings, and importantly, establish its empirical foundation. They follow this creative integration and coherent distillation of ideas with a clear articulation of what SBT means when the doors are closed facing the dilemmas of human existence. The evocative client examples come to life and provide understandable guidelines for conducting strengths-based therapy. They examine SBT in ways that it has never been examined or articulated before, its many strands of theoretical features woven together to create a tapestry of understanding; and its many tributaries of practice that flow together to merge into a common river of strengths-based practice.

Considering all the attributes of this book—the authors' clinical experience of doing SBT as well as their history of championing a non-pathological perspective, its cogent theoretical framework and empirical foundation, and its lucid guidelines of how to do SBT in encounters with clients—doesn't do it justice in terms of its contribution and why I consider it the one book I want everyone in the field to read. This book not only provides a scholarly yet immediately practical guide to SBT while eviscerating a pathology-based view, it elevates SBT beyond just another approach to add to the already too many flavors of the month. This book demonstrates that being strength based is transtheoretical and can be applied across clients as part of any practice of any model. It is a way of inhabiting any of the wonderful plurality of approaches available today. Please take whatever you can from this book and know that you are continuing the revolution of SBT these authors have not only advanced, but evolved to a new place of conceptualization and practice.

> Barry L. Duncan
> BetterOutcomesNow.com
> Jensen Beach, FL

Preface

We have good news and bad news. The good news is we know more than we ever have about helping people change. Decades of scientific research confirm that the most effective clinicians—regardless of theoretical orientation—"bring out the best in clients" by involving them in every aspect of therapy and privileging their strengths, perceptions, and feedback. Every idea and technique in this book is driven by these findings, which is why *practitioners of all persuasions can benefit from integrating SBT into their everyday practice*.

Now for the bad news. Despite empirical evidence linking therapeutic outcomes to the quality of client involvement and the therapeutic alliance, mental health services as a whole remain steeped in the medical model and out of step with the evidence. In contrast to traditional diagnostic-prescriptive approaches in which expert therapists analyze client deficits and prescribe corrective treatments, SBT clinicians build collaborative solutions inspired by client strengths, feedback, and other resources.

The book consists of 30 short chapters addressing SBT's key theoretical features (Part 1) and practical features (Part 2). Chapters in Part 1 present SBT as a transtheoretical, client-directed, culturally responsive approach that treats clients as resourceful heroes of change. In addition to highlighting the centrality of clients, Part 1 emphasizes the "person of the therapist" as a powerful therapeutic factor and offers guidelines for maximizing one's effectiveness as a clinician. The practical implications of SBT's theoretical features are woven throughout Part 1 to enhance theory-to-practice connections and applications.

Part 2 offers dozens of concrete techniques to help you put SBT into action on the job the very next day. Techniques in this section include being respectfully curious, instilling hope, recruiting client resources, using between-session strategies, and collecting systematic client feedback that gives clients a voice and choice throughout their care. The last few chapters of the book invite readers to "think outside the therapy room" by creating strengths-based work environments, integrating SBT into training and supervision, and acting for social justice.

We wrote the book for current and prospective mental health practitioners—psychotherapists, counselors, social workers, psychiatrists, graduate students, and anyone else in the business of helping people change. We use the terms therapy/counseling and therapist/counselor to align with the title of the book series, though we realize there are many other terms that could be used for therapeutic services and providers (social worker, helper, etc.). We use the word "clients" to refer to individuals, couples, or families.

Since people learn best from examples, the book is full of real-life dialogues from our work with individuals, couples, and families. While the names of clients have been altered for confidentiality purposes, many of the dialogues are lifted directly from session transcripts to provide an up-close-and-personal perspective of SBT in action.

Writing is a privilege and responsibility we take seriously. In an era of information explosion, time is precious and we thank you for including the book in your reading agenda. Our goal was to describe SBT ideas and methods in concise and practical ways that equip you to put the book into immediate action. We invite you to read on and judge for yourself whether we accomplished this goal.

Acknowledgments

We are grateful to many people for their inspiration, support, and contributions to our work. The following colleagues have significantly influenced our understanding and development of client-directed, strengths-based practices (listed alphabetically)—Harlene Anderson, Insoo Kim Berg, Harry Goolishian, Steve de Shazer, Barry Duncan, Michael Lambert, and Michael White. We offer special thanks to our friend and colleague Barry Duncan, who wrote the Foreword to this book and continues to inspire us through his tireless advocacy and efforts on behalf of client voice and choice in therapy. To Michael Lambert, Harlene Anderson, Michele Wiener-Davis, Arthur Bohart, and Mick Cooper, thank you for your wisdom and writings, and for your endorsement of this book. We also thank our partners and friends at the Heart and Soul of Change Project (www.heartandsoulofchange.com), an international repository of research, resources, and other information supporting the delivery of evidence-based, socially just therapeutic services to clients of all ages and circumstances.

To our students, thank you for helping us to continually question, learn, and refine our thinking, teaching, and writing. We appreciate the practitioners and trainers we've been privileged to supervise and consult with, whose wisdom, questions, and experiences have encouraged us to continue researching, revising, and writing about the challenges and joys of implementing collaborative, strengths-based practices.

We appreciate the proofreading assistance provided by Carley Owen, Greg Edgin, and other graduate students who read earlier drafts of the book. We thank our colleagues at the University of Central Arkansas and University of Rhode Island for their friendship, support, and collaboration on various projects over the years. To Joanne Forshaw, Senior Editor at Routledge Press, thank you for your support and professionalism throughout the book's writing and production. Jacqueline thanks Martin for his understanding and patience with her seemingly endless work, and Tricia, Tav, John, and Cary for their constant support. John thanks Deb for her love and patience, and Tom, Helen, Erin, Maura, Robbie, Ruby, and Julia for their ongoing reminders of life's goodness and possibilities.

Finally, we thank the individuals, couples, and families we have been privileged to work with. You remain our most reliable source of wisdom when it comes to delivering respectful and effective services.

Abbreviations

SBT	strengths-based therapy
SCF	systematic client feedback
PCOMS	Partners for Change Outcome Management System

Part 1

DISTINCTIVE THEORETICAL FEATURES OF SBT

History of SBT

Strengths-based therapy (SBT) is a client-directed approach that invites people to participate in every aspect of care and to apply their indigenous strengths and resources toward personally meaningful goals. As described below, SBT draws from a variety of sources, ideas, and methods.

Milton Erickson

Psychiatrist Milton Erickson practiced in the mid-1900s and died in 1980, but his pioneering ideas live on in the helping professions. The following ideas are particularly relevant to SBT: (a) clients are inherently resourceful and capable of changing, including those diagnosed with serious disorders; (b) the main reason to discuss past problems is to discover current resources; (c) clinicians should tailor services to each client; and (d) effective therapy helps clients discover and apply their natural strengths and resources. Consult the Erickson Foundation for additional information (www.ericksonfoundation.org).

Donald Clifton

Donald Clifton's work in the 1950s increased people's awareness of strengths-based ideas at a time when such ideas were rare. He was an educational psychologist who developed StrengthsFinder, an assessment tool that helps companies and individuals identify and apply their strengths. The American Psychological Association called Clifton the father of strengths-based psychology and the grandfather of positive psychology. Though not a therapist himself, Clifton's work solidified the theoretical foundations of SBT.

Social work

Strengths-based ideas are embedded in the writings of social worker Bertha Reynolds during the mid-1900s. Having observed the adverse effects of poverty and racial discrimination on the lives of her clients, Reynolds criticized the practice of "blaming the victim" by assigning psychiatric diagnoses to people who were reacting to oppressive social and political forces. Her influence is evident in the strengths-based principles of contemporary social work (Saleebey, 2013) and the social justice themes of SBT.

Counseling

The counseling profession has endorsed many strengths-based practices throughout its history. These practices include acknowledging client assets, emphasizing health and wellness, and advocating for socially just, culturally responsive services. Counseling organizations and scholars have repeatedly cautioned clinicians against diagnosing clients without carefully considering the impact of situational, developmental, sociocultural, and environmental factors (Sue & Sue, 2016).

Psychology

Psychological therapies have historically adopted a diagnostic-prescriptive approach to analyzing and correcting client difficulties. Recent proponents of positive psychology recommend greater attention to clients' strengths without minimizing their pain and struggles. Seligman, Rashid, and Parks (2006) note: "For over 100 years, psychotherapy has been where clients go to talk about their troubles, symptoms, traumas, wounds, deficits, and disorders.... In its emphasis on troubles, psychology... has seriously lagged behind in enhancing human positives.... Indeed, therapies that attend explicitly to the positives are few and far between" (pp. 774–775). SBT has also benefitted from the person-centered ideas of psychologist Carl Rogers, especially the emphasis on building strong client/therapist relationships.

Family therapy

Family therapy emerged in the 1950s as practitioners questioned intrapsychic approaches that minimized the influence of family and other social factors. Fueled by systemic theories from the UK and US, such as attachment theory (Bowlby, 1953) and cybernetic systems theory (Bateson, Jackson, Haley, & Weakland, 1956), family therapists operated from two main assumptions: (a) problems do not originate from within a person, but result largely from unproductive family communication patterns, and (b) family therapy produces more powerful and lasting changes than intrapsychic therapy. SBT and other systemic therapies have embraced the idea that problems do not automatically imply client pathology. More than just another treatment model, family therapy offered a new paradigm from which to approach clients, problems, and solutions.

Postmodern therapies

SBT borrows from postmodern approaches of the late twentieth century, all of which began as family therapies and were subsequently applied to individual and couple therapy. These approaches share the following assumptions and features: (a) there are many possible meanings or stories, versus one objective truth, that can be ascribed to clients and problems; (b) clients' personal meanings are shaped largely by the social contexts and conversations in which they participate; (c) therapeutic dialogue invites clients to consider alternate meanings and actions that help them achieve their goals; and (d) therapists collaborate with clients by accommodating their goals, preferences, and strengths.

Solution-focused therapy. Steve de Shazer and Insoo Kim Berg developed this approach in the 1980s based on their observation that clients can improve their lives without thoroughly understanding or discussing their problems (de Shazer, 1985; de Shazer, Berg, Lipchik, Nunnally, Molnar, Gingerich, & Wiener-Davis, 1986). Therapists help clients (a) describe a preferred future in which the problem is absent or less intrusive, and (b) increase "exceptions to the problem," referring to times when clients act in accordance with their preferred future. Drawing clients' attention to their successes enhances hope and provides tangible evidence that they can improve their lives. Refer to de Shazer et al. (2007) and www.sfbta.org for more information.

Narrative therapy. Developed by Michael White and David Epston in Australia and New Zealand (White & Epston, 1990), narrative therapists believe clients are deemed "problematic" when their opinions or actions do not fit the dominant preferences of groups or societies in which they participate. Guided by the notion that persons are distinct from the problems they experience, therapists help clients re-write their life stories by (a) critiquing the dominant social, cultural, and political norms against which clients evaluate themselves, (b) "externalizing" or reframing problems from internal pathologies to external influences and entities, and (c) helping clients change their relationship with problems and reclaim their lives. White (2007) elaborates on these and other features of narrative therapy.

Collaborative therapy. Originally called "collaborative language systems therapy" when developed by Harlene Anderson and Harry Goolishian (1992) in the United States and Tom Andersen (1992) in Norway, collaborative therapy maintains that the meanings we ascribe to events, experiences, and ourselves emerge largely from our social interactions and conversations. Problems result from narrow, inflexible dialogues within oneself and between oneself and others. Collaborative therapists adopt a position of "not knowing" in regard to clients—a relational stance that fosters new meanings and encourages clients to experiment with different ways of thinking and living. Like other postmodern therapies, this approach views clients as experts on themselves and trusts them to apply therapeutic conversations in ways that are uniquely useful to them. Consult Anderson and Gehart (2007) for more information.

Pluralistic therapy. Pluralistic therapy, developed in the United Kingdom by Mick Cooper and John McLeod (Cooper & McLeod, 2011), urges clinicians to approach clients, treatment methods, and therapeutic conversations with an openness and flexibility that allows for tailoring therapy to each client rather than imposing one's pre-established beliefs and techniques onto clients. By encountering clients from a position of "unknowing" (Spinelli, 2015), pluralistic clinicians are willing to be challenged and influenced by clients, and to employ a wide range of theoretical ideas and methods to accommodate each client's unique circumstances, goals, and response to treatment. Refer to Cooper and Dryden (2016) for additional information.

Feminist-influenced therapies. Feminist-influenced approaches view individuals within their sociocultural contexts based on the notion that psychological problems, especially those experienced by women and other marginalized groups, often reflect political and sociocultural injustices rather than individual pathologies (Hill, 1998). Client problems frequently result from the lack of social power, and clinicians promote egalitarian relationships in which clients assume active roles in shaping therapeutic content and goals. We view these as important considerations for *all* clients, not just women and other non-dominant groups.

Client-directed, outcome-informed (CDOI) practice

CDOI practice, originally called client-directed practice by Barry Duncan and colleagues (Duncan, Solovey, & Rusk, 1992), integrates client resources into treatment, collects systematic client feedback, and gives clients a central voice in therapy—all of which are core aspects of SBT. CDOI practice is not another model of therapy, but a set of transtheoretical values that enable clinicians of all orientations to improve services by putting clients first throughout the helping process. See Duncan (2014) and https://heartandsoulofchange.com for more information.

Recovery movement

The recent mental health recovery movement or "recovery model" has roots in many countries. This consumer-led movement maintains that all persons with mental health challenges are capable of living dignified lives despite their diagnoses and difficulties (Ramon, Healy, & Renouf, 2007). The movement draws from studies of the World Health Organization showing high rates of recovery from schizophrenia and other major struggles, and from personal testimonies of persons who have recovered from significant challenges. Recovery-based services build on people's strengths and help them recruit local, natural support systems such as family, friends, and community resources. As the name implies, the recovery movement is more of a philosophy than a therapeutic method.

In summary, SBT borrows from the innovative ideas and methods of many individuals, disciplines, and approaches. The next chapter describes how SBT blends these influences into a flexible set of therapeutic attitudes and actions.

SBT as transtheoretical and value added

SBT is a transtheoretical and value-added approach, meaning it can be applied to all clients by practitioners of all theoretical orientations to benefit whatever else is done in therapy. This chapter describes the core aim and features of SBT, along with common misunderstandings about strengths-based practice.

Core aim and features of SBT

The core aim of SBT is captured in two words—*client involvement*. Client involvement, also called client participation or engagement, refers to the extent to which clients participate in and contribute to therapy. SBT clinicians encourage client involvement by being client directed and alliance minded.

Client directed. SBT privileges clients' perspectives and involves them in every aspect of therapy. Duncan and colleagues (Duncan et al., 1992) coined the term "client directed" to operationalize empirical findings on common factors of change, which indicate that therapeutic success depends largely on the activation of common elements of helping that operate regardless of the therapist's specific treatment model or theory (Lambert, 2013). These elements include clients' resources, expectations, and perceptions of the client/therapist alliance. Of all such elements, *client factors* are the most powerful by far. Client factors consist of everything clients bring to therapy, which includes their unique strengths, wisdom, resilience, hopes, life experiences, cultural heritage, values, social supports, and ideas about what might help them. The extent to which clinicians incorporate these elements into therapy strongly impacts outcomes (Duncan, 2014). Common factors research provides compelling empirical support for putting clients at center stage by accommodating their strengths, feedback, and preferences.

Alliance minded. To say therapy is a relational process is stating the obvious, but we do so because the medical model continues to influence mental health professions in ways that can dehumanize those involved and minimize the importance of the client/therapist alliance (Elkins, 2016). The medical formula of diagnosing problems and prescribing treatments works well for broken bones, but not so well for therapy and counseling. Research repeatedly points to clients, therapists, and their alliance as the most potent ingredients of successful therapy (Wampold & Imel, 2015). It follows that the most effective practitioners are those who establish strong alliances, recruit client resources, and involve clients in every aspect of care.

One reason SBT appeals to practitioners is that its methods enhance the overall effectiveness of services regardless of one's theoretical orientation. For example, a therapist of any orientation who routinely collects client feedback and adjusts services accordingly will be more effective than one who does not do so. Like other methods of SBT, feedback enlists clients as partners in the change process (alliance minded) and gives them an ongoing voice in shaping services (client directed). The transtheoretical, value-added quality of SBT enables practitioners of all persuasions to add strengths-based practices to their therapeutic repertoire without abandoning other methods that are helpful to clients.

Misunderstandings of "strengths-based"

When presented as a specific treatment model or theory, strengths-based practice has been criticized for assuming people have everything they need to resolve every problem they face. This naïve assumption is not part of our SBT approach because it disrespects the complexity of clients and their struggles. SBT customizes therapy to each client, which often involves skill-building activities relevant to the client's preferences and goals.

Two other inaccuracies about strengths-based practices are that they lack empirical support and they rush clients into discussing strengths before acknowledging their pain and problems. Nothing could be further from the truth. First, every technique in this book is based on research findings related to common factors of effective therapy. Second, SBT is invitational rather than dictatorial; it meets clients where they are and never pressures them into discussing strengths (or anything else) without their consent. As an additional safeguard, SBT collects session-by-session feedback from clients to give them an ongoing voice in therapy and guard against imposing the therapist's preferred ideas or techniques.

Implications for SBT

This book invites you to view and apply SBT as a flexible framework of practice rather than a restrictive model of therapy. Practitioners of all theoretical orientations can improve their outcomes by implementing the client-directed, alliance-minded principles and practices of SBT.

3

Clients as heroes of change

Hero is not a word that typically comes to mind when thinking about people in counseling. In fact, clients may be viewed as *non-heroic*—anxious, dysfunctional, misguided, and the like. The literature related to common factors, client agency, and client resiliency turns this familiar narrative on its head. SBT honors the heroic qualities of clients and invites practitioners to rewrite the therapy drama by casting clients in leading roles.

Client/life factors

Derived from meta-analytic and comparative outcome research, common factors are those elements shared by all legitimate psychotherapy approaches. Psychotherapy is effective not because of how approaches differ, but because of what they share (Wampold, 2001). 86% of psychotherapy outcome can be attributed to client/life factors—those aspects specific to the client and incidental to the treatment delivered (Duncan, 2014; Lambert, 2013)—that is, anything having to do with the client and his or her life that aid in recovery apart from participation in therapy. The portion of outcome variance attributable to clients far outweighs any other common factor, including therapist and alliance effects.

Client/life factors include client motivations, a supportive family or community, or previous strategies for dealing with dilemmas. They also involve serendipitous events in clients' lives that create favorable conditions for recovery. For example, a counselor struggled with helping a family reduce conflict involving their teenage son, Luke. Luke's persistent refusal to follow rules, get ready for school, and do homework added to the family's stress of dealing with long commutes, a hostile landlord, and an unsafe neighborhood. Following several months of no change, the family moved into a small home in a new school district closer to the parents' work. They returned to counseling with a new outlook and described their excitement working together on their new home. Luke was attending school and family arguments were far less frequent. The counselor immediately focused on their new ways of interacting, helping them take hold and flourish. She recognized the critical importance of client/life factors and believed in the family's ability to capitalize on the change in their life circumstances, resolve their biggest complaints, and maintain those gains over time.

Clients as active participants

Instead of blank slates, clients actively shape the therapy process. For example, they redirect unhelpful therapists or modify therapist blunders to make services work for them (Bohart & Tallman, 2010). Bohart and Wade (2013) describe how clients fit therapist activities to their unique goals and preferences. Between therapy sessions, therapists' interventions trigger clients' generativity, including personal reflection, self-questioning, and preparation for sessions to promote change.

Clients also actively participate in alliance-building. They may express vulnerability to elicit therapist empathy, willingly self-reveal to enhance connection, or engage in prosocial behaviors such as humor and accommodation (Bohart & Wade, 2013). The therapy alliance, from this perspective, is a product of therapist *and* client activities. Clients', not therapists', perceptions of the alliance are the best predictors of outcome (Bohart & Tallman, 2010; Duncan, 2014). Rather than being distorted by pathology, clients' views accurately reflect their connection to their therapist and therapy process.

Client resiliency

Research repeatedly indicates that many people are able to self-right and heal, even following significant trauma. One study reported that only 5%–10% of persons exposed to some type of trauma developed significant posttraumatic stress; the rest moved forward without major life disruption (Ozer, Best, Lipsey & Weiss, 2008). Gurin (1990) similarly found that 90% of people who experienced significant health, emotional, addiction, or lifestyle problems in the prior year reported success in dealing with these difficulties. Many people who do not seek professional help successfully use methods similar to those employed by psychotherapists to restore well-being (e.g., re-exposure after trauma) without formal knowledge of what they are doing (Bohart & Tallman, 2010).

Even for conditions considered chronic and lifelong, recovery is not only possible but common (Bohart & Tallman, 2010). Research has shown an 88% recovery rate for people diagnosed with the borderline personality disorder over a 10-year period (Zanarini, Frankenburg, Hennen, Reich, & Silk, 2006). In a study of people experiencing a first psychotic episode treated with the open dialogue approach (Seikkula et al., 2006), 79% were asymptomatic at 5 years and 80% were either working, in school, or looking for work; the majority did not take medications. The idea that the more difficult the problem, the longer and more arduous the recovery, is not scientifically supported. Sudden, significant transformation is well documented and far more common than one would think (Bohart & Tallman, 2010). Prochaska, Norcross, and DiClemente (1994) conclude that, in or out of therapy, all change is self-change; therapy change simply has the benefit of a coach.

Shifting perception

Research on resiliency and other client/life factors invites a shift in perspective regarding clients' roles in counseling. Seeing clients as heroes requires knowledge of and a willingness to believe in the evidence. Like familiar figure/ground drawings, adopting a non-dominant view takes time. Once clients are seen as strong and resourceful, their strengths are more easily recognized. SBT endorses this perspective, not simply because it makes counseling more enjoyable, but because it capitalizes on the powerful role clients play in their own change and increases the likelihood of success.

4

SBT as client directed

Client-directed clinicians value clients' strengths, recognizing them as keys to success; they have faith that clients have invaluable insight into the issues that concern them and how they may be resolved. They put that faith to the test by reversing the traditional therapist/client hierarchy, putting clients at the forefront of the clinical process and their own change. Client-directed practitioners honor clients' goals and perspectives and use these to structure all therapeutic work. They do this, not simply because they value client strengths, but because empirical evidence shows that client-directed activities improve outcomes.

Origins

The term "client-directed practice" was introduced by Duncan, et al. (1992), followed by Duncan and Moynihan (1994). These authors postulated the crucial link between common factors and being client directed—specifically, research pointing to the prominent roles clients and the alliance play in psychotherapy outcomes. They argued that traditional approaches emphasizing therapist expertise outside the context of the alliance are empirically misguided. Instead, therapists who activate client potential and honor client preferences capitalize on key common factors. Thus, they called for the intentional use of *client*, not therapist, theories to tailor treatment goals and methods. Several approaches influenced the development of client-directed work. First, collaborative language systems conceptualized therapy as a conversation in which the therapist unfolds the client's story and meaning is continuously negotiated (Anderson & Goolishian, 1988); this process results in change. Therapists take a "not knowing" stance and consider clients to be the experts in their own lives (Anderson & Goolishian, 1992). Second, solution-focused therapy tailored all treatment strategies to client goals and preferences, acknowledging the importance of client resourcefulness. de Shazer (1988) commented that "[the] client constructs his or her own solutions based on his or her own resources and successes" (p. 50). Finally, narrative therapy (e.g., White & Epston, 1990) emphasized client local knowledge; clients' unique understandings of their lived experience take precedence over professional interpretations, including formal diagnosis and pre-determined intervention.

Client directed is not to be confused with client centered, the term coined by Carl Rogers (1951). While Rogers advocated that therapists attend to the client's frame of reference, he believed numerous techniques to be pivotal in bringing about change (e.g., use of reflecting statements). He viewed client problems through a lens of personality incongruence and his techniques and theory were considered appropriate for *all* clients. Thus, Rogers' client-centered approach is essentially therapist-centered—therapists operate from a specific theoretical foundation of client dysfunction and implement a corresponding approach despite each client's personal view of the problem and possible solutions.

The idea that therapeutic work ought to be client, not theory or therapist, directed was the conceptual linchpin for the development of formal feedback systems that routinely elicit client views of therapy. For example, the Partners for Change Outcome Management System (PCOMS) invites clients to expand their views, correct therapist misunderstandings, and collaboratively participate with counselors in continuously revising the direction of therapy (Duncan & Reese, 2015). In this way, clients' perspectives are integral to the direction of therapy.

What client directed isn't

Being client directed does not negate years of training in various methods; nor are client-directed therapists passive followers. Since clients generally *expect and want* therapists to offer novel perspectives and directions, client-directed therapists must have well-honed sets of skills to bring to the table. They should actively direct when this is what clients prefer.

Being a skilled clinician *and* client directed are not incompatible. To illustrate, a therapist who valued client strengths met with a family referred by social services. She listened attentively, commented on their strengths, and focused on developing a trusting relationship with each person. Despite these strengths-based, client-directed methods, she felt something was missing, confirmed when both parents rated the therapy alliance as weak at the end of the second meeting. One parent asked pointedly, "When are we going to start doing therapy, like on Dr. Phil?" This jolted the counselor out of the belief that empathic listening and joining would be sufficient for *all* clients! Inquiring further, the counselor learned that the family expected activities during meetings that would teach new skills. After apologizing for "not moving fast enough," the counselor assured them that such activities would be introduced at the next meeting. Not surprisingly, alliance ratings improved and stayed high after the therapist followed the family's lead and included structured communication activities in subsequent sessions.

Working with this family required shifting from a therapist-directed to a client-directed position. The therapist avoided the "bump on a log" syndrome—the notion that being strengths based and client directed entails simply sitting, listening, and nodding. While some clients respond well to such actions, the literature indicates that many clients complain about therapist inactivity and lack of direction (e. g., Anker, Sparks, Duncan, Owen, & Stapnes, 2011). Therapists are client directed when they assume the role preferred by the client.

"Leading from one step behind"

Being client directed can be summed up as an intentional stance of valuing client leadership in all therapy endeavors. This does not diminish the role of therapist expertise, nor does it ignore client wishes for therapist leadership. The phrase "leading from one step behind" perhaps best describes this seemingly paradoxical stance:

> *The therapist has an ethical obligation to be an expert and a knower in reference to his/her professional stance ... continually expanding his/her competencies, etc. But when s/he sits before the unique reality of another person or persons, s/he is truly a non-expert and a not-knower in the context of the client's developing new meanings*
> *(Cantwell & Holmes, 1994, p. 20)*

SBT therapists attempt to balance their expertise with the client's. Leading from one step behind is a creative and sometimes surprising process that activates client resourcefulness.

5

SBT and therapist factors

SBT emphasizes the importance of clients' strengths and resources in the success of therapy. However, therapists are not passive followers. Their ability to provide a context for bringing client resources to the forefront enhances success. Therapist effects are second in importance only to client/life factors in psychotherapy outcome. Therapist variation in overall effectiveness is well established (Baldwin & Imel, 2013). In other words, *who* the therapist is matters a great deal. This chapter addresses the question, "What makes some therapists more effective than others and how does this connect with SBT?"

Therapist effects

Client/life factors encompass all aspects of clients' lives, including personal, family, and community resources and difficulties. These factors account for 86% of the variance in therapy outcomes (Duncan, 2014; Lambert, 2013). In comparison, therapist effects account for 5% to 7% of outcome variance, with some research showing as much as 8% (Baldwin & Imel, 2013; Duncan, 2014). Therapist effects on overall outcome of treatment may seem modest, but when considering factors solely related to the treatment being delivered, therapists account for as much as 36% to 57%, more than any other factor (5 to 8 times greater than model differences) (Duncan, 2014).

Maximizing therapist effects

Despite evidence that therapists essentially *are* the treatment, psychotherapy's longstanding fascination with specific techniques has overshadowed their role. Popular manualized approaches require counselors to follow pre-set protocols of approved treatments for specific disorders. From this standpoint, therapists should minimize the natural back and forth of counseling conversations, focusing instead on priming clients to follow a prescribed treatment. Variations in treatment protocol and adaptations to client idiosyncrasies are discouraged. However, evidence suggests that the best therapists are not puppets to pre-specified techniques but work with clients in spontaneous and nuanced ways. Therapists who adapt to clients' worldviews, circumstances, and preferences are more likely to engage and be more effective with them. These therapists bring their humanity, including their struggles, into the counseling process to galvanize strong alliances and harness clients' resources and motivations.

Empirical evidence for the preeminent role of clients in the change process and their natural propensities toward resilience and creativity supports the shift from deficit-based to strengths-based perspectives (e.g., Bohart & Wade, 2013; Duncan, 2014). SBT therapists are skilled at setting the stage for client leadership and harnessing clients' full potential. SBT therapists:

1 believe that clients have strengths;
2 elicit client strengths;
3 incorporate client strengths.

Eliciting and incorporating client strengths operationalizes a strengths-based philosophy. Orlinsky, Rønnestad, and Willutzki (2004) state that "the quality of the patient's [*sic*] participation . . . [emerges] as the most important determinant of outcome" (p. 324). While therapist discipline, years of experience, and gender have not been found to be associated with improved outcomes (Beutler et al., 2004), evidence is emerging that resource-based attitudes and activities may engage clients more readily and result in better outcomes. In a study of 30 clients over 120 sessions, the most successful therapists identified and channeled client resources, while unsuccessful therapists focused on client problems (Gassman &

Grawe, 2006). The researchers suggested that their findings support *resource activation* versus *problem activation* in counseling. Another study of 296 clients in outpatient counseling found that a "growing sense of self-esteem in the interaction with the therapist" was the strongest predictor of whether clients stayed in counseling or dropped out (Kegel & Flückiger, 2014, p. 383). Clients who feel supported and empowered are more likely to participate in therapy.

Implications for SBT

It may come as no surprise that empirical evidence supports strengths-based practice given that clients are likely to invest in a process in which they believe they are valued and accorded a sense of agency. Working *with* clients is apt to be more satisfying than working against them, and having faith that clients can succeed is more energizing than viewing them as deficient. Collaborating with clients is no different than collaborating on any challenging endeavors—teamwork enlivens the process and maximizes success.

6

SBT and the therapeutic alliance

Counselors across all orientations place a premium on establishing strong bonds with their clients, regardless of whether they see this as setting the stage for intervention or as intervention itself (Norcross, 2010). An examination of the empirical evidence provides a basis for how focusing on client strengths fosters and maintains strong therapeutic alliances.

Empirical evidence for the alliance

Common factors research. The therapeutic alliance is responsible for as much as 36% to 50% of the outcome variance of therapy, over five times more than specific techniques (Lambert, 2013). Norcross & Wampold (2011) affirmed that "[the] therapy relationship makes substantial and consistent contributions to psychotherapy outcome independent of the specific type of treatment" (pp. 423–424).

Components of the alliance. When you ask clients what worked for them in their counseling, they routinely describe relationship variables, not techniques (Norcross, 2010). Clients report that therapists who listen with interest to their problems, offer encouragement, and instill hope, are helpful (Norcross, 2010). Therapist characteristics such as warmth and friendliness are mentioned frequently as important to successful therapy. In a qualitative study six months after couple therapy, respondents frequently cited similar therapist qualities as desirable (Anker et al., 2011)). However, many of these clients also stated that they wished their therapist had more actively structured sessions and provided useable advice for their daily lives.

The importance of relationship *and* task components are consistent with Bordin's (1979) classic three-part definition of the therapeutic alliance—client and therapist felt connection, client/therapist agreement on goals, and client/therapist agreement on tasks. Client and therapist felt connection involves such qualities as genuineness, empathy, and positive regard, first described by Carl Rogers (1951). These manifest in good listening and honest, empathic responses to client stories. Part of the client/therapist positive connection appears also to consist of the therapist's expression of positivity toward the client. Therapists who blame or attack have poorer outcomes than therapists who affirm (Najavits & Strupp, 1994). Kegel and Flückiger (2014) similarly found that an increase in clients' self-esteem resulting from their interaction with the therapist was the strongest predictor of successful therapy. Successful therapeutic bonds result when the counselor has and expresses respect for clients' concerns and faith in their ability to address them.

Agreement on goals involves counselors and clients being on the same page regarding the purpose and direction of counseling. Agreement on tasks requires synchrony between clients and therapists on the specific approach being used, and a shared faith that treatment will be successful. Hatcher and Barends (1996) identified *confident collaboration*—"the sense of committed participation in a helpful, hopeful process with the therapist"—as a key aspect of the alliance (p. 1334). Mild expressions of disagreement by clients regarding goals and tasks improved outcomes; strong alliances allowed clients to voice concerns and therapists the chance to address them. Along with agreement on goals and tasks and a positive therapist/client connection, confident collaboration results in a strong "working alliance" (Bordin, 1979, p. 252), considered the most powerful predictor of client retention and outcome (Horvath, Del Re, Flückiger, & Symonds, 2011).

Alliance monitoring and repair. As most counselors will attest, the alliance ebbs and flows throughout the course of treatment (Barber, Muran, McCarthy, & Keefe, 2013). Early alliance problems can result in negative outcomes (Norcross, 2010). Knowing when the alliance is at risk is crucial to preventing dropouts and poor outcomes. Research indicates that clients' assessments of the alliance more accurately predict alliance status than therapist or observer ratings, leading to the recommendation that therapists routinely collect client-rated alliance feedback (Horvath et al., 2011). A counselor's desire to learn if the alliance is off-track actually can strengthen the alliance (Hatcher & Barends, 1996). Prompting clients to share any discomfort about their therapist, as difficult as it may be, can remediate alliance ruptures and redirect the process in ways that enhance client participation. Alliance feedback conversations can help tailor interventions to client preferences.

Implications for SBT

Valuing clients' strengths is the foundation of SBT. Strengths-based therapists: (a) express a positive attitude about client potential and worth; (b) seek out and respect clients' preferences for goals, approaches, and content; and (c) incorporate formal client feedback and adjust treatment accordingly. These principles align with empirical findings of what constitutes effective therapeutic alliances and fosters meaningful client engagement.

7

SBT and hope

Hope is defined here as clients' anticipation of change (expectancy) and confidence in their ability to reach goals (self-efficacy).

Hope is a powerful common factor

Hope is a powerful element of therapeutic change regardless of one's treatment approach (Wampold & Imel, 2015). Some have even argued that treatment models achieve their effects largely through the activation of hope (Hubble, Duncan, Miller, & Wampold, 2010). In the classic book, *Persuasion and Healing*, Julia and Jerome Frank note that most clients enter services in a state of demoralization, and that the instillation of hope is one of the most important tasks of therapy (Frank & Frank, 1991). SBT "re-moralizes" clients by conveying that they are capable of changing, and they already possess valuable resources that can enhance their growth and change.

The power of hope is also supported by research on the *placebo effect*, a term that originated in drug research. The placebo effect occurs when people who receive a sham drug or placebo—a pill that resembles the actual drug but lacks any active chemical ingredients—feel better than people who receive nothing and often as good as those who receive the real drug. The placebo effect has been consistently observed in medicine and other forms of health care, including psychotherapy (Kirsch, 2010). These findings support the simple conclusion that people who expect to improve usually do.

Hopeful clients not only expect change to occur, but attribute positive changes to *their* efforts and actions. In a series of self-efficacy experiments, Dweck and colleagues found that people who linked achievements to their own strengths and actions were more likely to sustain their effort and successes than were people who attributed achievements to other factors (Dweck & Master, 2008; Molden & Dweck, 2006). These studies support SBT's attribution of therapeutic improvements to clients' efforts and actions through questions such as, "How did you improve things with your husband?" and "Where do you find the strength to keep going?"

Hope is fuel for action

When it comes to solving problems and reaching goals, hope is the fuel for effective action. Just as fuel-powered cars require gasoline to run properly and move forward, clients require an ample amount of hope to take action on their problems and goals. Unfortunately, the burden of serious problems diminishes clients' hope (Murphy, 2015). Given that people typically try to resolve problems on their own before seeking formal help, it is safe to say clients struggle for weeks or months before entering therapy. All these factors compound clients' demoralization and discouragement.

Consider Rochelle, an adolescent who lived in several foster homes and experienced a history of behavior problems in school and community settings. Problems included physical aggression, petty theft, school truancy, and running away from home. When asked how these problems affected her, she said, "It's like being stuck in quicksand. As soon as I pull myself up, something happens and down I go. No matter what I do, I always end up where I started. So what's the use?" Rochelle's statement vividly captures the way ongoing problems can chip away—one failure at a time—at one's hope, energy, and motivation. It's no wonder Rochelle, like others who struggle with chronic problems, feel rather hopeless and defeated by the time they enter therapy; the last thing they need from a therapist is yet another reminder of what is wrong or lacking in their lives.

One way SBT instills hope is by asking resilience and coping questions. For example, the counselor asked Rochelle, "With all you've been through, what keeps you from giving up altogether?" Rochelle cited various personal and social resources that helped her persist in the face of challenges, such as her "stubbornness," encouragement from her grandmother, and the support of a friend. In addition to revealing several strengths and resources that were integrated into change strategies in her treatment plan, this conversation instilled hope and revitalized Rochelle's commitment to improve her life.

Implications for SBT

As seen with Rochelle, SBT boosts clients' hope by recognizing their resources without denying their pain. But the benefits of hope are not limited to clients. One study found that counselors who focused on clients' strengths were more hopeful and less prone to burnout than those who focused on deficits (Snyder, Michael, & Cheavens, 1999). In addition to boosting the hope of clients, SBT clinicians nourish their own hope by having faith in people's ability to change and in the helping process itself.

8

SBT and social constructionism

SBT is guided by social constructionism theory. This theory maintains that people do not have direct or complete access to objective truth and reality, and that perceptions and knowledge about oneself and the world are personal constructions shaped less by objective discovery and more by sociocultural/linguistic creation (Gergen, 2009). This postmodern perspective distinguishes SBT from modernist approaches that assume people can directly experience and describe objective truths.

According to social constructionism, clients' personal, internalized constructions about themselves and the world result largely from direct conversations and indirect sociocultural messages. Regardless of where the messages originate—family, friends, teachers, religious leaders, television, movies, or books, for example—they are reinforced in clients' social relationships and interactions. Examples include: Boys are tough and girls are docile; homosexuality is a disease or sin; some races and cultures are inferior. When harmful messages are internalized, they become part of clients' personal realities, affecting them in ways that support depression, anxiety, or other difficulties. Shapiro, Friedberg, and Bardenstein (2006) describe the pervasive influence of personal constructions in the following way:

The personal meanings and stories that people construct make an important difference to their quality of life experience—for better or worse. Such filters affect the individual's self-concept, . . . understanding of her past, . . . and behavior in the future, because we behave in accordance with what we believe to be possible.

(pp. 137–138)

From a constructionist standpoint, ideas and theories about a client or problem are just that—ideas and theories constructed by people, *not* the one and only truth. To go one step further, the designation of a situation as a "problem" is itself a construction. While SBT clinicians cannot control clients' social interactions or the personal constructions that result from them, they can (a) consider the impact of social-linguistic factors on clients and their struggles, and (b) invite clients to embrace strengths-based, empowering perspectives of themselves and their possibilities.

Consider the impact of social-linguistic factors

The helping professions have traditionally viewed clients as having or being a problem ("he has ADHD," "she's a borderline"), which fuses problems with clients' identities in ways that diminish their hope and promote despair and defensiveness (Murphy, 2015). Social constructionism invites therapists to move beyond narrow diagnostic descriptions and embrace broader perspectives that enhance change. Discussing a problem within its larger context can reveal specific ways in which implicit, taken-for-granted assumptions of the dominant culture support the problem. These discussions are particularly helpful to clients who attribute problems solely to their own shortcomings and deficiencies, a view that limits hope and confines solutions to individually-based interventions such as medication or individual therapy.

Clients are often relieved and energized by the idea that the problem may not reside strictly within themselves. The SBT notion that perceptions of oneself and one's problems are influenced by cultural and social narratives—and are *not* direct representations of objective reality—allows clients and practitioners to flexibly adopt interpretations based on their pragmatic utility in promoting change rather than their presumed truth. This practical feature enhances the flexibility and appeal of SBT for therapists of all orientations.

Invite clients to embrace strengths-based, empowering perspectives

In addition to considering how social relationships and communications outside the therapy room have affected clients and their struggles, therapists can initiate strengths-based conversations that empower clients and enhance change. Social cognition research supports the idea that therapeutic discussions impact clients' hopes and self-perceptions in ways that mirror such discussions (Fiske & Taylor, 2008). For example, when people were asked to reflect on problems and other negative aspects of their lives, they reported lower levels of self-esteem and happiness than those who reflected on positive aspects and attributes (McGuire & McGuire, 1996). In another study involving 30 clients with a variety of problems, Gassman and Grawe (2006) found that unsuccessful therapists focused more on problems and less on strengths, while successful therapists made frequent and explicit efforts to identify client strengths and apply them toward therapeutic goals. These findings, in conjunction with social constructionism theory, support SBT's contention that therapeutic conversations can, for better or worse, strongly influence clients' self-perceptions, hopes, and outcomes.

Implications for SBT

SBT endorses the constructionist idea that clients' self-perceptions and hopes are strongly affected by social relationships, messages, and conversations. This perspective urges clinicians to (a) consider the influence of key relationships and messages in clients' lives, (b) use change-focused questions and language, and (c) invite clients to adopt hopeful perspectives of themselves and their prospects. In addition to empowering clients with the idea that they are not one and the same with their problems, the theory of social constructionism boosts practitioners' faith in the change-promoting power of therapeutic dialogue.

9

SBT language and practices

While practitioners may want to replace deficit-based practices with SBT in their work settings, they may encounter hard-wired obstacles. Typical mental health settings involve a gamut of procedures and documents that focus largely on client dysfunction. These include supervision conversations, staff trainings, and the various materials that comprise clinical work (e.g., brochures, electronic health records, treatment plans, and progress notes). These don't simply reflect practice, they influence what clients and therapists think and do. Like fish in water, clinicians are so immersed in this environment, they rarely perceive how it influences perception and clinical practice. Consequently, they may not evaluate their influence or consider alternatives.

This chapter gives readers a chance to re-view "mental health" as a unique culture. Re-configuring mental health to align with the empirical and philosophical underpinnings of SBT must begin with a critical evaluation of everyday policies and procedures. Then specific steps can be devised to create strengths-based practice environments.

Critical theory

"Mental health" denotes the commonplace, taken-for-granted body of practices that make up all aspects of psychotherapy (e.g., procedures, paperwork, policies). This infrastructure lies outside awareness and operates as an invisible constraint to alternative ways to think about and provide services. Making "mental health" visible requires "exoticizing the domestic," or making the commonplace newly strange (Bourdieu, 1988, xi). When this occurs, the strange and different draws attention and invites curiosity about how it operates and its effects. Two theories help make "mental health" visible, and, as a consequence, open for revision. These are social constructionism and discourse theory.

Social constructionism. Social constructionism theory asserts that humans build their understanding of the world through social interaction. Gergen (1985) claimed that social constructionism is concerned with "explicating the processes by which people come to describe, explain, or otherwise account for the world (including themselves) in which they live" (p. 266). This places meaning squarely in the realm of language. Language involves not only face-to-face talk but all communicative behaviors that explain what mental health is and what roles practitioners should play. From this standpoint, mental health theories and practices are not objectively "out there" but constructed through agreements among participants in conversation. As such, presumed truths about mental health reflect the cultural mores and social hierarchies of conversation participants.

Discourse theory. According to discourse theory, the experience of our everyday lives is shaped by discourses that support the norms of dominant classes (Foucault, 1972; Ricoeur, 1981). Discourse is a set of beliefs, statements, and practices that tell us what is true, who we are, and how we are to live in the world. Discourses derive prescriptive power from their invisibility. For example, clinician-generated assessments and treatment plans are rarely questioned in professional circles; they fly by perceptual radars undetected. On the other hand, discourses that advocate for more client-directed procedures stand out and become subject to debate as outside the mainstream.

"Mental health" constitutes a discourse—a range of practices and doctrines culturally entrenched and extending beyond the bounds of clinics and classrooms into daily lives. Amplified by the Internet and other media, it pronounces who is healthy and how to "treat the mentally ill." For example, TV ads for antidepressants or other psychiatric drugs infiltrate the consciousness of professionals and consumers, imparting a host of "truths" about what "mental illness" is, and what must be done to cure it. Saturation of such messages forms beliefs about "mental health," including that it is scientifically based, objective, and benevolent.

Discourse theory particularly focuses on how the creation of unexamined assumptions constructs relationships of power. In "mental health," expert knowledge, including knowledge to determine the true nature of the problem and the best way to resolve it, define a particular hierarchy in the therapist/client relationship. These power dynamics may not always serve the intentions and needs of service users. The first step in changing such practices is to identify them. This entails reassessment of the daily tasks of therapy. New procedures can then be developed that create more egalitarian client/counselor relationships and increase the voice and choice of those receiving services.

Implications for SBT

Power hierarchies constructed by certain practices inhibit the full partnership of client and clinician and the potential for client strengths and resources to be fully activated. Assessments that do not involve joint discussions of client views of problems, treatment plans that do not prioritize client goals and preferred methods, supervision discussions that exclude client feedback, and training that minimizes the importance of client collaboration impede the practice of SBT. Additionally, deficit-focused materials that fail to account for client strengths and the real constraints of clients' social contexts confound efforts to be resource-based. A critical assessment of one's own worksite and corresponding modifications of policies and procedures can gradually transform mental health "business as usual." In this new environment, clients are privileged in all aspects of service provision.

10

SBT and diagnosis

The popularity of psychological diagnosis (hereafter "diagnosis") is a source of wonder and concern in light of empirical evidence on how psychotherapy works and what makes it effective. This chapter describes several reasons why diagnosis is a poor fit for SBT.

Diagnosis lacks reliability and validity

Critics have repeatedly pointed out that diagnosis lacks sufficient reliability and validity—two essential criteria for any assessment procedure. Diagnostic reliability reflects the extent to which different clinicians agree on a client's diagnosis. The fact that clinicians cannot consistently agree on clients' diagnoses based on independent evaluations is indicative of significant reliability problems (Carson, 1997; Kirk & Kutchins, 1992). Authors of the newest *Diagnostic and Statistical Manual for Mental Disorders* (DSM-5; American Psychiatric Association, 2013) claim that it is "the cornerstone of substantial progress in reliability" (p. 5), while critics point out that the reliability estimates for the *DSM-5* field trials are statistically inflated and, for all practical purposes, have not improved since 1974 (Frances, 2012; Vanheule et al., 2014). Some of the harshest criticisms of diagnosis have come from the very people who know it best. For example, *DSM-III* developer Robert Spitzer acknowledged the unreliability of diagnosis by saying "if you're in a situation with a general clinician it's certainly not very good" and that "it's not clear how to solve the problem" (Spiegel, 2005, p. 63).

Validity refers to the extent to which an assessment procedure measures what it purports to measure. Diagnostic systems in psychotherapy, such as the *DSM* and *ICD* (International Classification of Diseases; World Health Organization, 2004), claim to measure specific, discreet disorders that allow clinicians to distinguish between the disorders themselves and between the disorders and normal developmental or situational challenges. Neither system lives up to this claim. The fact that reliability is a prerequisite of validity and that diagnosis is highly unreliable explains why diagnosis suffers serious validity problems. For example, critics have long established that DSM diagnoses contain significant overlap with one another, are often indistinguishable from everyday human behavior, and not identify specific or discreet conditions. Simply put, diagnosis fails the crucial test of validity—the ability to represent and delineate conditions that actually exist (e.g., Caplan, 1995; Kendall & Zablansky, 2003; Kirk & Kutchins, 1992). A 2002 DSM report reinforces this point by stating that "the goal of validating these syndromes and discovering common etiologies has remained elusive . . . not one laboratory marker has been found to be specific in identifying any of the DSM-defined syndromes" (Kupfer, First, & Regier, 2002, p. xviii). Allen Frances, lead editor of the *DSM-IV*, offers a more candid opinion of the validity problem: "There is no definition of a mental disorder. It's bullshit. I mean, you just can't define it" (Greenberg, 2010, p. 1).

Diagnosis is not applicable or helpful in SBT

Given its reliability and validity problems, it is no surprise that diagnosis has fallen short on its original promise to help clinicians select effective treatments. Diagnosis is based on the medical assumption that effective treatment requires accurate diagnosis. This assumption is helpful in repairing broken bones and treating physical ailments, but it is not helpful in psychotherapy because therapy works differently than surgery and other medical procedures. More specifically, the diagnostic-prescriptive equation of "expert assessment (diagnosis) + specific treatment (prescription) = cure" overlooks the powerful role of the client, the therapeutic alliance, and other common factors of change that determine the effectiveness and outcomes of therapy. Simply put, diagnosis does not provide useful information for helping clients change.

Diagnosis locates problems within clients

Diagnostic systems assume problems originate and reside primarily within the persons who experience them. This narrow viewpoint contrasts sharply with SBT's systemic emphasis on the impact of socio-cultural factors on clients' struggles and solutions. These systemic factors play a key role in every aspect of SBT.

When therapists view clients' problems as symptoms of internal pathology or deficits, they may naturally limit treatment options to "internal" ones such as medication or individual therapy while excluding potentially useful social/environmental strategies such as altering clients' interpersonal interactions or social environments. For example, if a teacher or parent believes a child's attentional difficulties result from a biological deficit, they may logically assume medication is the only reasonable treatment and fail to consider how changes in the child's home and school environment might support successful behavior (Maag, 2018). In this sense, diagnosis may reduce clients' and caregivers' accountability, creativity, and persistence in developing commonsense solutions. Diagnosis also reinforces a one-dimensional, totalizing self-image in which clients begin to view *themselves* as the problem ("I am ADHD"). By attaching problems to those who experience them, diagnosis works against SBT's empowering, multi-dimensional view of clients.

Implications for SBT

For reasons noted above, SBT views diagnosis as unnecessary and potentially harmful to the change process. The deficit-based assumptions and actions of diagnosis clash with SBT's emphasis on client strengths and possibilities. When diagnosis becomes a taken-for-granted element of mental health services, clinicians and clients may begin to accept it as fact rather than interpretation.

SBT fully acknowledges the reality and pain of serious problems, and does not minimize the possibility that some clients may experience a sense of relief from having a name for their struggle. However, SBT clinicians also recognize that diagnosis represents only *one* of many possible stories about clients and their lives. Diagnosis magnifies the deficit-based story, but strengths-based stories are also available. These stories co-exist for all clients, and clinicians have the choice of which ones to accentuate in therapeutic conversations. In SBT, the choice is a pragmatic one based on the question, "Of all available stories, which ones are most likely to activate common factors of change and thereby improve outcomes?". Outcome research on common factors (Lambert, 2013) and therapist focus (Gassman & Grawe, 2006) strongly favors stories of strength and competency over stories of failure and deficiency.

11

SBT as systemic

Prior to the 1950s, psychotherapy relied heavily on Freudian principles; the individual's private inner world was the territory of interest. The emergence of systems theory in the mid-twentieth century offered an alternative. Viewing individuals as inseparable from their social contexts took hold and opened new vistas for intervening. Systems theory continues to be widely used in many current psychotherapies. Its primary principles provide a coherent theoretical base for SBT.

Origins and principles

Systemic theory derives from two primary sources: general systems (von Bertalanffy, 1968) and cybernetics (Weiner, 1948). Both hold that human processes are best understood by analyzing mutually influential relationships. General systems theory challenged scientific reductionism of the early twentieth century. Instead of believing that phenomena are ideally explained by examining discreet components, it claimed that correct understanding involves how components interact with one another. The concept of wholeness asserts that phenomena are not simply a collection of discreet parts, but a patterned set of interactions—thus the classic phrase "the whole is greater than the sum of its parts." Systems consist of complex organizational properties such as boundaries and hierarchies.

Cybernetics was the brainchild of mathematician and engineer Norbert Weiner (1948). Weiner attempted to unify diverse understandings of living and non-living systems by adapting concepts from communications engineering, specifically information, feedback, and homeostasis. He asserted that social organization operates like an information-processing machine, collecting and using information to perform critical functions. However, he claimed that unlike machines, humans learn; they are capable of transforming their organization according to information input. In other words, a system's balance (homeostasis) can transform (morphostasis) into a different system depending on maturational or environmental inputs that trigger change.

In the development of *ecological systems theory* Bronfenbrenner (1979) expanded general systems theory to include relationships among systems. He was interested in networks of systems, particularly connections between the family and larger social units such as neighborhoods, communities, and cultures. The same mechanisms governing families apply to how relationships structure communication between each of these levels, impacting the well-being of an individual.

Implications for SBT

Systems theories provide several platforms that support SBT. First, they are concerned with the complex social factors surrounding a client's problem, not just intrinsic biological or psychological causes. This invites assessment of interactional patterns in the client's social world. The problem is not the client's alone but is shared by key participants in a social network. This broadened view can reduce clients' negative self-assessments and therapists' deficit-based attributions.

Second, locating the problem in an interpersonal domain offers a range of possible solutions not otherwise available. Approaches that target the client's significant social relationships promote flexible treatment strategies that mobilize client hope and engagement.

Third, a systems perspective implies that the problem may be a product of, or at least exacerbated by, societal forces. People's social location (e.g., class, race, ethnicity, gender, religion, or sexual preference) has a significant impact on their functioning and possibilities. For example, an adolescent in trouble in a poor neighborhood starts from a place of disadvantage compared to one from the "right side of town." Understanding clients' social locations contextualizes their struggles and sets the stage for a more realistic and empowering therapy.

Finally, systems theory offers a rationale for how such difficulties might be addressed in therapy. For example, a therapist working with a delinquent adolescent could ask a local mechanic if he is willing to apprentice the youth. Or, a neighborhood church group may offer him safe, affordable social activities. The saying "it takes a village" applies here; solutions depend on the activation of local knowledge and resources, with the therapist but one member of the client's helping team.

Limitations

Systems theory's compelling explanatory power has garnered scores of devotees dedicated to applying its tenets to every situation and every client. This can be a significant pitfall for SBT or any other approach. Systems theory is one of many potential ways to make sense of the dilemmas clients present. Its principles are not universal and may not fit for all clients. SBT counselors are primarily interested in aligning their practices with their clients' worldviews. The tendency to use systems theory as a one-size-fits-all explanation can inadvertently devalue clients' own meanings, alienating them from the therapy process and compromising the alliance. Instead, SBT therapists can honor and work within clients' worldviews, offering alternatives tentatively.

Contextualizing clients' problems in systemic terms can also suggest that clients are helpless in the face of intractable forces. To suggest to a child that her phobias are related to her parents' drinking, or to a recent immigrant that his anxiety is a result of society's reaction to him, may inadvertently provoke greater despair. Despite barriers beyond clients' or therapists' immediate control, SBT therapists can collaborate with clients to create plans that promote personal agency.

On the other hand, classic systems theory historically has been critiqued for *not* attending to power differentials. For example, feminists have pointed out that circular causality, a general systems concept based on a view of the reciprocal nature of cause/effect interactions, obscures male-generated violence in intimate relationships and positions women as equally responsible for their abuse. SBT therapists can recognize the relativity embedded in classic systems theory, and strive to promote accountable and safe relationships.

Finally, systems theory is not a panacea for overly pessimistic attitudes in the psychotherapy arena. Indeed, most of the early applications of the theory focused on family dysfunction. Experts were still the experts and clients were still labeled, albeit for defective communication or relationships with significant others. SBT uses a systemic lens to locate strengths within relationships and to broaden therapy to include the ideas, energies, and hopes of significant others in the client's life.

Cultural considerations in SBT

The term *culture* is used here to refer to everything that impacts and distinguishes a person, such as one's race, age, gender, sexual orientation, immigration and colonization experiences, and family heritage. Every client brings a unique blend of cultural influences to therapy. These influences may promote strength, pride, oppression, or challenge, depending on the client and situation. Sociocultural factors can create and sustain clients' problems. This point applies to all clients, but is particularly relevant to those from underrepresented groups such as persons living in poverty, LGBTQ clients, women, persons of color, and clients with developmental disabilities. For example, the depression or anxiety experienced by clients from non-dominant populations may result largely from ongoing exposure to invalidating messages that they are inferior to persons from dominant groups.

Challenges of providing culturally responsive services

The fact that most helping professionals are from dominant groups adds to the challenge of providing culturally responsive services. Mental health practice has historically been a White, middle-class activity that embraces Western values such as individualism, self-reliance, and autonomy (Ivey, Ivey, & Zalaquett, 2014). The individual-centered perspective of Western psychotherapy sees problems as residing primarily within the client and encourages treatments that emphasize self-exploration, self-management, and the individualistic pursuit of goals. While this may work for some clients, it fails to acknowledge the impact of discrimination and other contextual factors that adversely affect clients, as well as other methods of healing and problem solving that may fit better with a client's preferences and cultural/familial background. These problems help explain why most traditional therapies have failed with clients from non-dominant groups (Sue & Zane, 2006).

Unfortunately, well-intentioned efforts to improve clinicians' cultural effectiveness may perpetuate the very problems they seek to resolve. For example, cultural competency training often requires people to memorize customs and traits of various cultural groups. This may raise awareness about cultural diversity, but it undermines the complexity of people and reinforces the stereotyped notion that *everyone* from a particular ethnic group shares similar characteristics. Other aspects of traditional cultural competency training have been criticized for (a) implying that counselors can achieve cultural competency through intellectual knowledge and awareness, (b) focusing on client-related cultural factors with little attention to counselor factors or to counselor–client power disparities, and (c) implying by the word "competency" that it is somehow possible for a counselor to achieve full mastery of culture-related knowledge and skills.

We prefer the term *cultural humility* (Tervalon & Murray-García, 1998) to cultural competency because it more accurately describes the stance of SBT practitioners in relation to clients. As noted by Hook, Davis, Owen, Worthington Jr., and Utsey (2013), culturally humble therapists "rarely assume competence" and "approach clients with respectful openness" (p. 354).

In discussing clients of color, Ridley (2005) cautioned clinicians against stereotyping by emphasizing that "each client is unique . . . and each has a different story to tell" (p. 85). Others have similarly noted the dangers of typecasting clients and losing sight of individual differences based strictly on race, diagnosis, or other incomplete descriptions of a client (Boyd-Franklin, Cleek, Wofsy, & Mundy, 2013; Sue & Sue, 2016). The following comments of a graduate student capture these concerns and propose a sensible solution:

> *What we're mostly talking about in the classroom . . . is stereotypical representations of different ethnic groups—"this is a*

> *typical Latino, this is a typical Vietnamese person," but each individual is different, no matter what their race. I think what we should try to develop is a curriculum that exposes people to a new way of thinking, to help them approach all people with an open mindset.*
>
> *(Sleek, 1998, p. 1)*

Implications for SBT

This section summarizes three ways SBT clinicians enhance the cultural responsiveness of their services.

1. View every client as a culture of one and every session as a cross-cultural exchange. SBT therapists accommodate cultural differences among clients, and between clients and themselves, by viewing every client as a *culture of one* and every meeting as a *cross-cultural exchange*. They approach clients much like a foreign ambassador would approach an unfamiliar culture (Murphy, 2015) —by asking, listening, and learning about who clients are, what they want from services, and how their strengths and resources might help them achieve their goals.

These collaborative ideas differ sharply from authoritarian approaches where clinicians diagnose problems and prescribe treatments with minimal client input. It is no surprise that underrepresented clients frequently report power disparities in the client/ counselor relationship (Chang & Yoon, 2011). Clients who view themselves as inferior to their counselors display less therapeutic engagement and hope than those who experience collaborative, egalitarian relationships (Balmforth, 2006). SBT counselors promote client engagement and hope by approaching every client from a position of cultural humility as evidenced in the following practices:

- Acknowledge the inability to fully understand clients' experiences and the need to learn from them in order to be helpful.
- Approach clients with a "beginner's mind" that conveys respectful curiosity.

- Treat clients as collaborators and experts on themselves.
- Adapt therapeutic interventions to fit clients' preferences and circumstances.

2. Involve clients in every aspect of their care. One of the most common recommendations of scholars who research cultural issues in counseling is to involve clients in their care to the extent that they are able and willing to participate (Sue & Sue, 2016). Effective alliances and outcomes depend largely on the degree to which clients participate in shaping therapeutic goals and tasks (Wampold & Imel, 2015). Ridley (2005) notes that many under-represented clients "enter counseling feeling powerless" and "gain a sense of empowerment and ownership of the counseling process when they participate in their own goal setting" (p. 107). Honoring the goals, resources, and feedback of clients is a hallmark of strengths-based practice.

3. Identify and apply client strengths and resources. Building on client strengths and resources is a fundamental feature of SBT and culturally responsive services. As Ridley (2005) points out, "While vigorously looking for psychopathology... counselors often miss opportunities to help clients identify their assets and use these assets advantageously" (p. 103). In counseling with non-Western clients, Pedersen (2000) urges clinicians to help clients apply their own internal resources and self-corrective mechanisms because this is a common method of problem solving in non-Western cultures. Boyd-Franklin et al. (2013) similarly advocate a strengths-based approach for African American clients who are often more aware of their weaknesses than their strengths. We have found this to be true of most clients regardless of their race and cultural background.

13

Social justice and SBT

While there are many definitions of social justice, all address the impact of "social institutions, political and economic systems, and government structures that perpetuate unfair practices, structures, and policies in terms of accessibility, resources distribution, and human rights" (Vera & Speight, 2003, p. 254). According to Vera & Speight (2003), discrimination and prejudice are quality-of-life issues negatively impacting people of color, women, gay, lesbian, transgender, and other marginalized people in society. Having a social justice perspective in psychotherapy entails recognizing that many problems clients present are related to the effects of injustice. This chapter proposes that SBT's attention to context, shared power, and clients' strengths helps to counteract oppressive conditions faced by socially oppressed clients and provides justification for political engagement by practitioners.

Focus on context

SBT centers what clients bring to therapy, including extra-therapeutic factors. Class, immigration status, gender, race, religion, and other social dimensions can enhance or inhibit clients' chances of achieving life objectives. For example, it is easier for a parent with access to quality childcare to parent effectively than for someone working two jobs who relies on a neighbor for childcare. Similarly, feeling unsafe in one's neighborhood can induce anxiety and impact a client's self-worth, making it difficult to accomplish basic life tasks. SBT therapists take into account the social ecology of clients' lives and how it restricts options for problem resolution or may, in fact, *be* the problem.

Understanding the role of social context in clients presenting concerns draws into question many traditional assessments focused on intrapsychic or biologic causes. This perspective suggests, for example, that diagnostic labels do not provide an adequate basis for fully-informed treatment plans that account for a client's social ecology. Individually-focused explanations for problems situated in difficult social conditions can inadvertently blame clients and distract from mobilizing client strengths and addressing societal constraints. SBT therapists honor clients' descriptions while assessing imbalances in resources and privilege as ways to understand and address client problems.

Self-determination, strengths focus, and shared power

Central to a socially just society is the right to determine the course of one's life and having the means to do so. Traditional psychotherapy methods can unwittingly minimize clients' social locations as sources of distress. Resulting "treatment plans" construct roles of client as patient and therapist as healer, reinforcing social power hierarchies and diminishing clients' sense of personal agency. A strengths-based approach honors what clients bring to the table. Clients are seen as experts in their own lives and the rightful drivers of therapy. This value is embodied in the collaborative stance of SBT practitioners. Treatment planning and implementation are the result of mutual conversations from which new perspectives and solutions emerge.

The shared power of SBT may represent a radical departure from many clients' experiences with professional helpers, encouraging them to reassess how power operates in other relationships. Strengths-based conversations may inspire clients to demand inclusion in decisions that impact their well-being in multiple areas of their lives, including work and close relationships. Thus, SBT can have a ripple effect that reconfigures power across multiple domains of clients' lives. SBT's incorporation of systematic client feedback operationalizes shared power by communicating that the client's voice matters as meaningful, actionable data. Responding to client feedback means that SBT clinicians *do* social justice with each client at each meeting.

Social action

Helping clients experience a greater sense of agency and life satisfaction is a worthy enterprise. However, some have advocated that counselors actively address racism, poverty, sexism, and other sources of oppression linked to client distress. Prilleltensky (1999) stated that "there cannot be health in the absence of justice" (p. 99). Without efforts to eradicate injustice, therapy may actually support it. Martin Luther King Jr. warned that psychologists should not always help people "adjust" to what is because "there are some things in our society, some things in our world, to which we should never be adjusted," including, for example, racial discrimination and economic inequality (1968, p. 11). Simply helping clients feel better, with little attention to the role of injustice in contributing to distress, can give tacit approval to an oppressive society and mask the need for change.

Silence provides cover for oppression (Sue, 2001). When stories of prejudice and discrimination are buried in a therapy file, they cannot join other accounts to inspire social change. Martin Luther King Jr. stated that the link between peoples' wellbeing and their social positions "needs to be carefully documented [made known] and consequently more difficult to reject" (1968, p. 2). Though the contextual focus of SBT may increase clinicians' awareness of social inequities and inspire speaking out and engaging on broader political levels, the call for social action spans theoretical orientations.

Challenges

Many clients are impacted by longstanding unjust societal structures. This may help clients see their difficulties as not exclusively of their own making. While this may be liberating, it can engender a sense of hopelessness. For example, how does a young person trying to learn in a classroom with crumbling walls and outdated textbooks have hope for a prosperous future? It is important that SBT practitioners acknowledge the magnitude of certain inequities *and* communicate a belief that personal effort can make a difference. This may mean working collaboratively to locate community resources, encouraging client voice in relevant arenas, and/or exploring with clients the possibility of uniting with others to instigate change. It may also entail therapist involvement in building more equitable communities. SBT therapists know that social change is an ongoing challenge yet maintain unwavering faith in clients' abilities to thrive, even in the midst of oppression. They also view collective action as relational power that can lead to transformative change. Such work must be done from the ground up—clinicians are not saviors of the oppressed, but engage in political activism informed by views of those most affected (Goodman et al., 2004). As in SBT, local voices are the best sources for fashioning what type of help and efforts are most needed to address social injustice.

14

SBT and client feedback

Practitioners from various settings are increasingly using standardized instruments to collect client views of therapy to identify clients at risk of premature dropout and to adjust treatment accordingly (Duncan, 2014). The evidence that systematic client feedback (SCF) improves outcomes prompted the American Psychological Association to state that "ongoing monitoring of patient progress and adjustment of treatment as needed are essential" (APA Task Force, 2006, p. 280). SCF invites clients into full partnership with professionals and promotes their participation in their services—the most critical determinant of treatment outcome (Orlinsky, Rønnestad, & Willutzki, 2004).

Empirical foundation

SCF refers to the continuous monitoring of client perceptions of progress throughout therapy and a real-time comparison with an expected treatment response to gauge client progress and signal when change is not occurring as predicted (Howard, Moras, Brill, Martinovich, & Lutz, 1996). With this alert, clinicians and clients have an opportunity to shift focus, re-visit goals, or alter interventions before deterioration or dropout. Several feedback systems have emerged (Castonguay, Barkham, Lutz, & McAleavey, 2013), but only two have randomized clinical trial support and are included in the Substance Abuse and Mental Health Administration's (SAMHSA) National Registry of Evidence Based Programs and Practices (NREBP). The first is the Outcome Questionnaire-45.2

System (OQ; Lambert, 2010), designed to monitor client functioning at each session and meant to be used not only for research but as a clinical tool.

The second system included in the SAMHSA's NREBP is the Partners for Change Outcome Management System (PCOMS; Duncan & Reese, 2015). Derived from everyday clinical practice and specifically designed to privilege the client, PCOMS employs two standardized instruments with four items each. One measure assesses outcome (Outcome Rating Scale/ORS; Miller & Duncan, 2000) and the other assesses therapeutic alliance (Session Rating Scale/SRS; Miller, Duncan, & Johnson, 2002). PCOMS is the first system to directly involve clinicians and clients in a continuous process of measuring and discussing progress and the alliance.

In a meta-analytic review of six OQ System studies ($N = 6,151$), clients in the feedback condition had less than half the odds of experiencing deterioration and were approximately 2.6 times more likely to attain reliable improvement than those in treatment as usual (Lambert & Shimokawa, 2011). The same review evaluated three PCOMS studies ($N = 558$) and reported that clients in the feedback group had 3.5 times higher odds of experiencing reliable change and less than half the chance of deterioration. There are currently five randomized clinical trials conducted by the Heart and Soul of Change Project that support the efficacy of PCOMS in individual, couple, and group therapy (see https://heartandsoulofchange.com). Clients in feedback conditions were less likely to drop out and achieved more pre-post treatment gains, higher percentages of reliable and clinically significant change, and faster rates of change.

Of particular interest is how this evidence sheds light on how to do effective therapy. Expert assessments that specify a treatment path are replaced by an evolving process tailored continuously to conform to client preferences and expectations. How to approach each therapy encounter cannot be predicted ahead of time but must be learned one client at a time as each brings his or her unique attributes, concerns, and preferences to the therapy endeavor (Duncan, 2014).

PCOMS and SBT

Consulting clients on a regular basis operationalizes an SBT perspective. While the use of client feedback in general is a step toward incorporating client strengths, PCOMS, in particular, embodies SBT in three primary ways:

1 *PCOMS is feasible*. Consisting of 4 analog scales, the measures require a minute or less to complete—the ORS at the beginning of the session and the SRS at the end. Lengthier feedback tools can be intimidating and perceived as wasting valuable meeting time, potentially dampening client participation in therapy. PCOMS' brevity fosters client engagement and makes it a very practical tool for real-world service environments.
2 *PCOMS has no predetermined content categories*. Instead of detailed, expert-derived checklists, clients simply place a mark on a line indicating their score on 4 broad life domains for the ORS and general aspects of the alliance on the SRS. The open-ended nature of the instruments allows clients to freely reflect on and express their unique experience.
3 *PCOMS is collaborative*. Once clients score the instruments, counselors invite them to discuss them—a key feature that distinguishes PCOMS from other CFSs. This is a fundamental reversal of the expert/client hierarchy, privileging *client* interpretations and meanings. The collaborative conversation that follows the client's ratings provides an idiosyncratic snapshot of the client's concerns, goals, and preferences.

PCOMS thus represents a realistic way to enact a client-centered, collaborative, and strengths-based philosophy.

15

Challenges of SBT practice

Implementing SBT can be very difficult because it requires significant perceptual and behavioral changes on the part of mental health practitioners and agencies. Before moving from SBT's theoretical features to practical techniques in Part 2, we want to discuss four challenges encountered by practitioners who shift from deficit-based approaches to SBT, along with suggestions for addressing each challenge.

Challenge 1: Acknowledging strengths AND struggles

Practitioners of any therapy approach need to ensure that their allegiance to the approach does not override their commitment to client benefit and the therapeutic alliance. In strengths-based work, this can happen when clinicians zealously focus on strengths without properly acknowledging clients' pain and struggles. Our SBT approach advocates a *both-and perspective* in which therapists hear and validate all client stories—possibility and pain, strength and struggle, success and failure—rather than pressuring clients into discussing strengths before they are ready, or continuing to focus on strengths when clients indicate a preference for something different.

Clients respond best to compliments or other positive acknowledgments when they believe therapists understand their struggle. This understanding need not involve time-consuming explorations of problem history. It does, however, require careful attention to client preferences and a willingness to listen to the *whole* story, not just the parts about strengths.

Challenge 2: Being client directed

This challenge is based on a common misunderstanding of what it means to be client directed. Practitioners who are new to strengths-based practice sometimes misinterpret the client-directed component of SBT to mean that clinicians should listen to and validate clients, but should not offer suggestions. This may work for some clients, but not for those who prefer a more active therapist who provides advice and interventions. In contrast to nondirective approaches that dissuade clinicians from ever offering suggestions, SBT urges therapists to tailor their actions to each client's preferences.

When clients want direction and advice, SBT therapists provide it. To do otherwise would jeopardize the alliance. Any approach that places the practitioner's model over client preferences is not client directed. The surest way to sustain a client-directed focus in SBT is to obtain client feedback and adjust services accordingly.

Challenge 3: Linking strengths to outcomes

Practitioners who are new to SBT sometimes forget that identifying strengths is a means to an end, not an end in itself. For example, it is possible for a therapist and client to generate a long list of strengths with little attention to how those strengths relate to the client's goals. Discussions of strengths, like everything else in SBT, are linked to the client's goals and reasons for seeking services. Once therapists identify a strength, they explore if and how it may help clients reach their goals.

Challenge 4: Being persistent and patient

Shifting from deficit-based to strengths-based practice can be a long and difficult journey, which is why we encourage clinicians to be persistent and patient with themselves, their colleagues, and their agencies. Old habits are hard to break, and SBT requires a radical departure from clinical traditions that have dominated helping professions for over a century. For these reasons, we offer the following suggestions to clinicians and agencies wishing to incorporate SBT into everyday services.

Remember WHY you want to be strengths based. Reminding yourself of SBT's core values and principles will help you sustain the energy needed to become strengths based. Any significant change involves setbacks and obstacles. Clinicians and agencies who are solidly committed to the core values of SBT—giving clients a voice in services and privileging client resources—regularly remind themselves of these values as they face individual and organizational obstacles to becoming strengths based.

Take a strengths-based approach to becoming strengths based. Just as SBT invites clients to build on their resources, we advise clinicians and agencies to build on what they already have and already do to support strengths-based practices—existing personnel, ideas, actions, policies, and anything else that enhances the implementation of SBT. If you or your agency become exhausted or overwhelmed by trying to do too much too soon, take a short breather to celebrate how far you've already come in your SBT journey. Slow and steady usually beats fast and furious when it comes to implementing a new approach to service delivery, especially one that requires substantial changes to business as usual. On the upside, many clinicians who adopt SBT report a renewed sense of joy, vigor, and gratification. As they shift from therapist-directed to client-directed practice, they also experience relief from the high-pressure role of sole expert in the client/therapist relationship.

Enlist the help of others. Seek out opportunities to collaborate with like-minded colleagues in your agency, region, or profession through local and online discussion groups, webinars, workshops, and related activities. In addition to reading this book and similar sources, Chapter 29 offers a brief list of online resources related to SBT.

Enjoy the ride. Working with people who struggle with serious problems can be painful and frustrating as well as gratifying and enjoyable. Clients can tell whether we approach therapy as a burden or a joy. Effective therapists approach their work and clients with a respectful sense of humility, appreciation, and adventure. We recommend doing the same as you apply the ideas and methods of this book.

Part 2

DISTINCTIVE PRACTICAL FEATURES OF SBT

16

Being respectfully curious

The term *respectful curiosity* captures the unassuming relational attitude from which SBT clinicians approach clients. By adopting a position of "not knowing" (Anderson & Gehart, 2007) or "unknowing" (Spinelli, 2015), clinicians view every client as an unfamiliar *culture of one* and every therapeutic interaction as a *cross-cultural exchange*. An overarching attitude of humility and respect pervades every aspect of SBT. This chapter describes how SBT practitioners convey respectful curiosity throughout the helping process.

SBT therapists express respectful curiosity by assuming the role of learners and treating clients as experts on themselves and their lives. The success of SBT rests largely on therapists' ability to learn what clients want from therapy (hopes and goals) and bring to therapy (strengths and resources). The following examples illustrate the therapist's need to learn from the client:

- I need your help in order to be useful.
- Is it okay if I ask a few questions to learn more about this?
- I need your feedback about how our meetings are working for you.
- Can you help me learn more about your hopes of becoming a better parent?

Being respectfully curious honors the fact that therapists cannot effectively understand clients' experiences or determine what will help them without their active input and involvement. Rather than prescribing therapist-driven interventions from a position of superiority, SBT clinicians collaborate with clients to co-construct solutions based on clients' own ideas, feedback and resources. Respectful curiosity facilitates *collaborative, client-directed dialogue* that empowers clients to freely accept or reject any ideas and strategies that emerge from therapeutic conversations, including those offered by the therapist.

The following phrases illustrate how SBT clinicians incorporate the language of curiosity into the ideas and suggestions they offer clients:

- Could it be that . . . ?
- I'm wondering . . .
- Is it possible that . . . ?
- I'm not sure this will make sense to you, but . . .
- You can decide if this is worth considering, . . .

Cara's story

Cara's parents referred her to counseling due to concerns about school behavior, most of which revolved around Cara's argumentative behavior in her high school science class. The science teacher, Ms. Kraft, frequently redirected or reprimanded Cara during class. Interestingly, Ms. Kraft stated that Cara was capable of doing good work when she applied herself.

When asked for her take on the situation, Cara said, "Ms. Kraft is super strict. She gets onto me all the time about stupid stuff like homework and studying. She doesn't do that to other students. She just doesn't like me and she's out to get me." Cara continued, "Now my parents think there's something wrong with me. I understand that, because I get in a lot of trouble at school. But I'm not crazy or anything like that. I just treat others the way they treat me. If Ms. Kraft doesn't want me to act up, she needs to chill instead of giving me a hard time. She doesn't care about me, so why should I care about her?" Later in the conversation, Cara said she wanted to do better at school, to pass science class, and to move on to the next grade.

Cara's interpretation of her teacher's actions and motives appeared to perpetuate a repetitive, unproductive pattern of interactions that worked against her goal of passing class and improving school performance. In the next session, the SBT counselor offered a feasible but different interpretation that, if accepted, might disrupt the pattern and invite a different response (words and phrases of respectful curiosity are italicized):

> When we met last week, you were saying that Ms. Kraft was too strict and didn't care about you. *I'm wondering* if there *might be* any other *possible* explanations for her actions. *I'm not sure* if this makes any sense, but I'll let you decide since *you know the situation better than I do. Could it be* she gets on your case about homework and studying because she cares enough to say these things rather than ignoring it and making her life easier? After all, her life will go on pretty much as is regardless of whether or not you pass her class. *Is it possible* that reminding you about this stuff is her way of showing concern for you? *I don't know*, what do you think?

Cara was intrigued but cautious about accepting the new interpretation. After complimenting her for being open-minded enough to even consider a different view, the counselor and Cara collaborated on an experiment (it was science class, after all) in which Cara would carefully observe her interactions with Ms. Kraft for two weeks and pay close attention to Ms. Kraft's responses to her. Cara reported the results of the experiment in this way: "Maybe I was a little wrong about her, but she's still my meanest teacher." While things were far from perfect between Cara and Ms. Kraft during the remainder of the school year, she improved her school performance enough to pass science class and move to the next grade.

Cara's example illustrates an important premise of SBT and respectful curiosity: *How* we talk with clients is every bit as important as *what* we say to them. By using the language of respectful curiosity, the counselor offered a different view in an invitational rather than dictatorial manner. This gave Cara full freedom to accept or reject the different view on her own terms with no pressure from the counselor to justify or defend her choice. In addition to promoting collaboration and client involvement, respectful curiosity preserves clinicians' credibility when the client perceives their ideas or suggestions as inaccurate or unhelpful. For example, if a client rejects an idea presented as a "possibility" that "might help" rather than the one-and-only truth, then SBT clinicians simply move on with their credibility intact and no harm to the therapeutic alliance.

Respectful curiosity is client directed

One of biggest benefits of respectful curiosity is that it keeps the focus of SBT on the most powerful element of effective therapy—the client. For example, when clients improve, SBT therapists might ask, "What gave you the idea to try something different this time?" or "How did you resist the urge to do what you used to do?" These questions clarify how clients made improvements and empower them to take credit for their accomplishments.

To summarize, respectful curiosity is more of a stance or attitude than a specific technique. Being respectfully curious invites clients to view themselves as essential contributors to therapeutic change who are worthy of the therapist's genuine intrigue and wonder. As evidenced in the chapters that follow, respectful curiosity is the attitudinal and relational foundation of many SBT techniques.

17

Validating clients

Imagine struggling with a problem for several weeks before considering formal therapy. You are embarrassed by the problem and by your inability to resolve it. As you describe your struggle during the first session, the therapist's comments and questions compound your embarrassment because you experience them as evaluative and judgmental. This chapter helps clinicians avoid this scenario by validating clients instead of judging them.

SBT clinicians validate clients by respecting their concerns, accepting their experiences, and assuming they are doing the best they can under the circumstances—each of which "meets clients where they are" instead of implying they should be somewhere else or someone else (Duncan et al., 1992). As illustrated in the opening scenario, clients may be wary of clinicians' judgments because they are ashamed of the problem and of their inability to resolve it, both of which create defensiveness and distract them from their goals. Validation frees up clients to focus on building solutions rather than defending themselves. SBT clinicians validate clients by:

- listening to what clients say and how they say it;
- acknowledging and normalizing their concerns, feelings, and perceptions;
- conveying faith in their ability to change and grow;
- empowering their desire to change and ability to cope with difficult circumstances;
- integrating their unique strengths and resources into therapeutic conversations and interventions.

SBT clinicians use direct and indirect forms of validation. Indirect validation involves *minimal encouragers* (Cooper, 2016) such as head nods and brief comments like "yes," "uh huh," and "okay."

Direct forms of validation address specific aspects of the client's situation, feelings, and actions:

- I can see why it's important for you to speak up when people disrespect your family.
- With everything you've been through, I can see why you feel depressed. The bigger mystery for me is how you've managed to continue handling things at work and home.
- No wonder you're so anxious. This is a big and difficult decision for you.
- It makes perfect sense to take your time instead of rushing in and trying to fix everything all at once.
- You have every reason to feel this way.

As evidenced in these statements, validating clients' concerns and perceptions sends the message, "I accept you and your situation as is." When validating clients, SBT therapists refrain from verbal or nonverbal behaviors that convey judgment or criticism, such as frowning or asking clients why they feel or act the way they do. After all, solving problems is hard enough without having to defend oneself.

Liza's story

Liza was a university student who thought she was "going crazy" because of recent changes in mood and behavior that included frequent crying, skipping classes, and speaking rudely to her mother and friends. Liza looked very fatigued and distressed when she arrived for the first therapy session. She told the therapist her boyfriend of one year broke up with her by phone three weeks earlier. Her mother and friends were urging her to "get over it and move on," which was not helping according to Liza.

Liza: My mom and my friends keep telling me to move on and find someone else. They're probably right, but it's hard to do after a year with someone. I can't just "move on" like nothing happened.

Therapist:	That's understandable.
Liza:	We were together for almost a year. I still care about him. I know I should get over it but I can't. I cry all the time. It's affecting my school work, too. I don't feel like doing anything except sleeping and crying. I feel like I'm going crazy. It's scary.
Therapist:	No wonder you're so upset. You've been with someone you care about for a long time and then it ends all of a sudden. You have every reason to be scared.
Liza:	That's what I tell my mom and my friends, but they don't understand. I know they care and they're trying to help, but it's not helping.
Therapist:	It's hard to understand someone else when you're not standing in their shoes. It sounds like they care about you and want you to be happy. But you also want to make decisions when *you* are ready to make them.
Liza:	Exactly.

Phrases such as "no wonder you're so upset" and "you have every reason to be scared" validated Liza's struggles and perceptions, which in turn reduced her fear of "going crazy." She returned in two weeks for a second session looking more rested. Things were slowly improving in her personal life and at school. Liza decided to discontinue therapy with the understanding that she could return whenever she wished. She thanked the therapist for helping her. When asked what was most helpful, Liza said, "You listened and understood."

With some clients, as with Liza, validation may be all that's needed to unleash the inherent strengths needed to resolve a problem. With others, validation is part of a more extended process of collaborating with clients to develop therapeutic goals and implement other change strategies. Validating clients' perceptions and feelings does not require SBT clinicians to agree with them. The therapist's job is to help clients achieve their goals, not to convert them to a prescribed set of beliefs or actions. Validation in SBT frees clients from defending themselves and allows them to focus their full attention on building solutions and achieving goals.

18

Instilling hope

The installation of hope is woven into many aspects of SBT, from developing goals and recruiting client resources to attributing improvements to clients' efforts. While other chapters address many of these methods, this one focuses on two hope-instilling techniques in SBT—offering compliments and facilitating future-focused conversations.

Offering compliments

One of the simplest ways SBT clinicians instill hope is to compliment clients on strengths, accomplishments, and personal qualities. As illustrated in the following examples, compliments may be folded into statements or questions:

- Your kids are lucky to have such a caring parent in their corner.
- With everything going on in your life, it's impressive that you were able to get to work on time every day this week.
- Where do you find the courage to keep trying going rather than giving up?
- How did you manage to speak up for yourself despite being so nervous about it?

The very fact that clients are in therapy verifies their commitment to resolving problems and improving their lives. Thus, most clients can be genuinely complimented for attending sessions ("It takes courage to meet like this"), addressing problems ("Facing challenges is hard work"), cooperating with the counselor ("Thank you for being patient and answering my questions").

Even though some compliments are applicable to many clients, SBT practitioners tailor every compliment to the client's unique situation. Patrice was demoralized when she entered therapy with her two sons, both of whom were displaying behavior problems at home and school. She and her husband recently divorced and he was living in a different region. On top of all this, Patrice was caring for her grandmother and working two jobs to support the family. The following exchange occurred during the first session when Patrice appeared particularly discouraged.

Patrice: I don't know why I even bother sometimes.

Therapist: I can't imagine what this is like for you. These things would completely knock some people down, but here you are. How do you manage to stay at it and keep going?

Patrice: I'm a very strong-willed person. Some people call it "stubborn." [*smile*]

Therapist: So your strong will or stubbornness helps you stand up to these challenges instead of giving in to them.

Patrice: What choice do I have? I have to be there for my kids. I'm all they have.

Therapist: It's a good thing for them they have a strong parent like you.

Patrice: Thank you.

Therapist: What else helps you continue hanging in there and trying to make things better for you and your kids?

Patrice appreciated the therapist's recognition that she was doing *something* right for herself and her family—a hopeful message that counteracts demoralization and despair. The therapist and Patrice continued to discuss how her strong-willed attitude and other resources could help restore family harmony and stability. This example illustrates how compliments not only help to instill hope, but also set the stage for exploring client resources. In a study of the relationship between outcomes and specific elements of therapy, therapists' use of compliments correlated strongly with positive outcomes (Linssen & Kerzbeck, 2002). SBT clinicians put this finding into action by offering genuine compliments to clients throughout the course of counseling.

Facilitating future-focused conversations

Chronic problems have a way of hijacking hope and promoting deficit-based thinking on the part of clients and clinicians. If therapists focus on diagnosing and correcting deficits, then therapy becomes a past-focused effort to reduce what clients do not want in their lives. In contrast, SBT clinicians facilitate future-focused conversations that clarify what clients *want* from services (desired future) and what is already in place to help them achieve it (strengths and resources). The following discussion addresses the first part of this SBT equation.

The first session of SBT typically involves hearing and validating clients' concerns, then inviting them to describe their hoped-for future by asking questions such as:

- What are your best hopes for our meetings?
- What do you want from counseling?
- How will you know counseling is working?

Everything that happens in SBT from this point on addresses clients' answers to these questions. Since many people do not give much thought to future possibilities when embroiled in serious difficulties, SBT clinicians obtain specific details of clients' desired future—what it looks like, how they will know they're achieving it, and how its achievement will influence their overall quality of life. The following questions are helpful in this regard: "If you woke up tomorrow and had achieved your best hopes, what would be different?"; "If counseling ended and you were pleased with the results, what would be different in your life?"

Without denying the reality of clients' difficulties or rushing them into future-based dialogue before hearing and validating their concerns, future-focused conversations offer clients the rare opportunity to briefly step away from daily difficulties and describe what they want instead. SBT clinicians even approach problems in contextual, future-focused ways by discussing them as "obstacles" or "roadblocks" to a desired future rather than simply problems that need to be solved (Madsen & Gillespie, 2014).

SBT practitioners also instill hope by presuming change is inevitable. A *presupposition* implies something without directly saying it. SBT clinicians incorporate presuppositions into questions and conversations to convey confidence in the inevitability of change and in clients' ability to improve their lives. The italicized words in the following questions seek to instill hope by presupposing future changes in the client's situation:

- What *will* be the first small sign our meetings are working?
- How *will* you know *when* things are getting better between you and your son? What difference *will* that make in your relationship?
- Who *will* be least surprised *when* things start getting a little better?

Future-based words such as *will* and *when* convey faith in clients' ability to improve their lives. Consider Shawn, an adolescent referred by the school and legal system for chronic nonattendance of school. The judge ordered increased parental supervision, evening curfew, and counseling. The following exchange occurred two days after Shawn's court appearance:

Counselor: I read the court summary and I know there's a lot going on now. What would you like to see happen?
Shawn: People need to chill and back off, and stop treating me like a criminal. All I did was skip school. It's not like I murdered somebody.
Counselor: How will that make things different for you when people back off and chill a little?
Shawn: It'll be better. Is that what you mean?

Counselor: Yes. I'm just wondering how your life will be different with your relationships, home, school or anything else you can think of, when things start getting just a little better.

Shawn: I guess my parents won't ground me as much.

Counselor: What about school? How will school change when things start improving?

The counselor's presumption of change laid the groundwork for exploring what Shawn was willing to do to improve things at home and school. As it turns out, Shawn increased his school attendance enough for his parents, school, and the court system to "chill and back off" just as he had hoped.

19

Exploring clients' theories of change

In a first session, Lisa listened attentively as Mara described how her mood had worsened over the past months, and at times, even getting out of bed was difficult. She attributed her struggles to a discussion with her sister during which she remembered being abused by their father. Mara was convinced that resolving her depression would require "going back." Lisa ended the session by commenting on Mara's resilience. As homework, she asked Mara to note days when she was feeling somewhat better. Unfortunately, Mara failed to show for her next appointment and did not call to reschedule.

Typically, counselors have a preferred framework for understanding and addressing problems presented by clients in therapy. For example, Lisa followed what she believed to be a strengths-based formula to connect with Mara. In other instances, Lisa's empathic listening and future-focused homework would have resulted in the client's renewed hopefulness. However, in Mara's case, Lisa's approach did not fit the client's "theory of change."

First described by Duncan et al. (1992), the client's theory of change involves clients' ideas about their problems and what it will take to resolve them. These generally are not precise or fully formed theories, but are more like ballpark hunches. To access Mara's theory of change, Lisa could explore her intuitions about the source of her distress and possible paths to recovery. This might include discussing what Mara remembered about her past abuse and what she felt would help to alleviate her pain as well as the role she wants Lisa to play in therapy. Lisa then could translate Mara's views into relevant tasks such as asking her to journal her memories of the abuse. Discovering and integrating the client's theory of change in this way may have given Mara greater hope and increased the likelihood she would return for the next session.

Following the client's theory of change, even when it seemingly contradicts SBT principles (e.g., problem or past-focused theories) is, paradoxically, the essence of SBT. It communicates to clients that they are experts in their own lives and that their views matter most and contain the seeds of change. It also can improve client participation, a critical aspect of outcome. Clients who resonate with their counselor's approach are more likely to be engaged, and this is more likely to happen when counselors seek out and incorporate clients' theories. To summarize, honoring clients' theories of change:

- puts clients center stage;
- enlists client participation;
- enhances the therapeutic alliance;
- fosters egalitarian collaborations;
- provides structure for therapy conversations and activities.

Discovering clients' theories of change

Questions related to goals, change, possible solutions, and therapeutic approach all help clinicians explore and tap into clients' theories of change.

Goal questions:

- What do you think needs to happen for things to get better?
- What were you hoping would be different by meeting with me?
- What needs to happen for you to say we've been minimally successful in dealing with your concern/s?
- What do you want to change about your life/your problem?

Change questions:

- Have you been up against anything like this before? If so, what happened? How did it change/get better?

- How do you typically make changes in your life? Can you tell me about this?
- Who in your life might either help, or stand in the way, of your resolving this problem?
- Who in your life (past or present) would not be surprised to see you resolve this successfully? How would he/she say you will do this?

Solution questions:

- What have you tried so far that has helped even minimally to resolve this problem?
- What might you imagine would be a first step to begin to deal with this problem?

Approach questions:

- How can I be most helpful to you?
- Sometimes people want their counselor to be a sounding board. Others want specific advice or strategies. What do you prefer?"

By the end of the first session, a therapist should have at least an emerging picture of what clients want from therapy and the role they want the therapist to play. The second and third meetings can elaborate and confirm these, and routine check-ins in the form of systematic collection of client feedback ensures that clients' views guide the process.

Incorporating clients' theories of change

Once the counselor obtains a rudimentary idea about what the client is expecting or hoping for from therapy, s/he follows the maxim: "Just do it!" (Duncan & Sparks, 2010). Clients' theories of change are often broad starting points. It is the counselor's job to offer more concrete suggestions; it is the client's job to accept, reject, or help refine these. In the above example, Lisa could have offered the following:

> *It sounds like you believe that what happened to you as a child has a lot to do with how you are feeling now. If it makes sense to you, we could spend some time talking about that, of course letting you set the pace. A retrospective journal could be a way to get your thoughts down about your experience. We can continue to check in to see if this is helping, and, if it isn't, there are other avenues we can explore. How does that sound?*

The key here is to make sure the therapist's suggestions are one of several viable options, giving the client the power to shape the strategy. Mara might respond:

> *Yeah, I think that would help, but I don't want to feel worse. Maybe I could just write one entry and see how I feel.*

Lisa can then assure Mara that she can go at her own pace and that there are other ways to approach the problem if needed. The goal is to increase Mara's engagement and the expectation of improvement by tapping into her theory of change.

Honoring clients' theories of change capitalizes on client factors by highlighting knowledge about their own lives, fostering strong working alliances, and building hope for change. In order to realize these benefits, counselors must:

- privilege clients' views of the problem and solution over psychological theories;
- have an eclectic set of skills to fit a range of client preferences;
- check in regularly to make sure that the method matches clients' views and, if not, collaboratively strategize on a new plan.

20

Exploring clients' desired future

The truism "if you don't know where you're going you'll probably end up somewhere else" is as applicable to therapists as it is to travel agents and taxi drivers. Just as travel agents and cab drivers determine where people want to go before assisting them, SBT therapists learn where clients want to go before embarking on the therapeutic journey. This chapter illustrates how SBT clinicians help clients describe their desired future and develop goals or "next steps" toward that future.

Describing the desired future

Clarifying clients' desired future is one of several things that occur during the first couple sessions of SBT. Before inquiring about the desired future, SBT clinicians typically (a) explain the centrality of client input and preferences, and (b) administer the Outcome Rating Scale (ORS) to identify clients' key concerns and reasons for seeking therapy. These interactions set the stage for exploring clients' hoped-for future and developing therapeutic goals through the following actions.

Exploring what clients want from therapy. SBT places clients at center stage in determining the goals and focus of therapy. This process begins by discussing clients' ORS ratings and the reasons they are in therapy. SBT clinicians never rush clients into talking about future hopes before providing ample opportunity for them to describe the concerns that led them to therapy. To do otherwise jeopardizes the alliance and hinders outcomes. After learning about clients' concerns, SBT clinicians explore what they want from services by asking questions such as:

- What do you want most from therapy?
- How will you know our meetings are helpful?
- What are your biggest hopes from our counseling sessions?
- When we stop meeting like this, what will convince you our work was successful?

Whereas questions like "What brings you here today?" or "Why are you seeking therapy?" often elicit deficit-based descriptions of the past (what clients *do not want* or wish to move *away from*), the questions listed above invite clients to envision and describe hoped-for futures they *want* to move *toward* in their lives. Even when therapists frame questions to elicit a positively worded description of the desired future, clients may respond with problem-based descriptions of what they do not want. While this is understandable given that most people struggle with problems for quite a while before entering therapy, helping clients reduce an undesirable situation ("being less depressed") does not automatically lead to something desirable. When clients respond with negatively worded descriptions, SBT therapists ask what they would prefer *instead of* the undesired problem ("What would you prefer doing instead of being depressed?").

The following example illustrates a conversation with Emma, who was very distraught about recent arguments and apathy in her relationship with her partner, Michelle. Michelle's job schedule prevented her from attending therapy with Emma.

Therapist:	What do you want most from therapy?
Emma:	I want us to stop moping around and arguing so much.
Therapist:	Okay. What do you want to be doing *instead of* moping around and arguing?
Emma:	Being the way we used to be.
Therapist:	Which was . . . ?
Emma:	Kinder and more loving.

Detailing the desired future. Once SBT clinicians get a general sense of what clients want from therapy (a "kinder and more loving" relationship with Michelle), they obtain a more *specific description of the desired future* by asking the following types of questions:

- If you woke up tomorrow and your relationship with Michelle was just as you want it to be, what would you notice first? Then what?
- If we watched a movie of you and Michelle being kinder and more loving, what would we see?
- If it was three months from now and your relationship improved significantly, what specific signs would tell you things were better?

Therapist: If we watched a video of a kinder and more loving relationship, what would we see?
Emma: We'd be smiling and laughing more. We laughed a lot when we met, but not now.
Therapist: What else would indicate the relationship was improving?
Emma: We would go out more on weekends and do more fun things.
Therapist: Such as . . .?
Emma: Going to movies and restaurants, seeing friends. Stuff like that. [*Asking "what else" and "such as . . ." promotes a more thorough and concrete description of Emma's desired future*]

Most clients appreciate the opportunity to describe their hoped-for future and, with gentle urging, can do so in sufficient detail. Detailing Emma's desired future will help her to notice when it is happening and to gain encouragement from such observations. This discussion highlights SBT's social constructionist emphasis on the power of language and dialogue in that "as client and therapist talk more and more about the solution they want to construct together, they come to believe in the truth or reality of what they are talking about" (Berg & de Shazer, 1993, p. 9).

Detailing the desired future also involves clarifying its *influence on other areas of clients' lives*. Questions the therapist asked Emma for this purpose included "How does your hope for a more loving relationship tie into your overall values?" and "How will improving your relationship with Michelle impact other areas of life?" The opportunity to consider and respond to these questions motivates clients to sustain their pursuit of a better future. For example, Emma's response to the above questions helped her realize that improving her relationship with Michelle would (a) support her value of being "a source of light in the world," and (b) enhance her energy level, quality of sleep, and job performance. These realizations bolstered her commitment to the relationship and prompted several immediate actions that included writing occasional "love notes" to Michelle, planning more evenings out, and sharing jokes and stories during dinner.

Developing "next steps"

Once clients describe their desired future, SBT clinicians collaborate with them on developing "next steps" and actions ("What could you do *this week* to improve things with Michelle?"). For practitioners and agencies that use treatment plans, next steps can serve as clients' short-term goals in such plans. SBT goals flow directly from clients' desired future and typically share three features—positive, specific, and small. These features are evident in Emma's short-term goals, all of which addressed her hopes for a more loving relationship with Michelle. *Positive* goals describe actions clients will undertake to achieve more of what they want ("I'll say something kind to Michelle in the morning") rather than less of what they don't want ("I won't snap at Michelle as often"). The positive wording of goals is not imposed on clients if they indicate a different preference. However, positively worded goals generally are more invigorating and easier to observe than negatively stated goals such as "being less depressed." *Specific* goals break abstract intentions ("I'll be kinder") into concrete actions ("I'll ask Michelle if she needs help making dinner"). Specific goals enhance the structure and direction of therapy, and enable clients and clinicians to accurately monitor progress. *Small* goals are more achievable, and thus more effective, than large goals that may set clients up for failure. The SBT clinician invited Emma to consider a small goal by asking, "What is one small, manageable way you can show your love for Michelle this week?" Small changes often lead to larger ones, and the achievement of small goals helps clients sustain their hope and motivation. For these reasons, SBT favors small, doable goals ("Leave work by 5pm on Wednesdays to tidy up the kitchen before Michelle gets home") over larger, impractical ones ("Tidy up the house every evening").

The above goals served as tangible "next steps" toward a more loving relationship with Michelle. By the third and final session, the relationship was on the right track and Emma decided to discontinue therapy.

21

Recruiting client resources

The first step in recruiting client resources is to believe they have them. Without this, therapy is likely to proceed down a path that can heighten feelings of despair and diminish hope for change. However, when counselors believe that clients possess personal, community, and cultural resources, they are more likely to purposefully look, listen, and ask for them. You might say resources get a fair hearing. When this happens, untapped resources become visible and available.

Seeing and hearing resources

Believing leads to seeing. Consider the following scenario. You are doing a visit at the home of a mother with three children. The apartment where the family lives is small and plaster is beginning to peel from the walls. The mother, in robe and hair curlers, is propped on the couch on the phone when she yells for you to come in. You notice right away the half-eaten pizza on the coffee table, a baby in diapers crying in the playpen, and one toddler playing with spoons on the floor, perilously close to a knife next to the pizza and a cord dangling from a plugged-in iron atop an ironing board. Another child is curled asleep on a mat in the corner next to a space heater.

This is a caricature of what a counselor or social worker might encounter during a home visit. A deficit lens finds ample issues to worry about. When this is all one sees, resources become invisible. However, an SBT clinician's resource lens allows a new picture to emerge, one with the following "hidden jewels":

- The youngest child is in a playpen, indicating attention by the mother/caretaker to the child's safety while she is on the phone.
- Another child is sleeping, apparently contentedly, on a mat on the floor.
- A third child is playing with a wooden spoon.
- The pizza box indicates enough resources to provide at least a meagre meal.
- The mother/caretaker has curlers in her hair, suggesting care for her own appearance.
- The mother/caretaker is on the phone, indicating connection to others outside the family home, perhaps a friend or relative.
- Despite the apparent disrepair of the dwelling, pictures hang on the wall, revealing efforts to make the home a home.
- The TV is on, meaning up-to-date payment of the electricity bill.

Other resources can be spied (or deduced). Seeing even a few provides an opening for exploring whether they can be mobilized to address client concerns. Seeing resources in this way does not negate the importance of recognizing and responding to problems, especially those concerning the safety and well-being of children, but it *also* allows strengths to be a part of building solutions.

Seeing resources occurs in less dramatic fashion in daily clinical practice. A depressed woman shows up for her weekly appointment with a surprising purple-dyed streak in her hair. Or a 13-year-old "problem child" momentarily rests her head on her mother's shoulder. These, and others like them, reveal exceptions (Chapter 24) and invite respectful curiosity about their meaning. Opportunities to highlight and harness client resources also occur in client and therapist conversations. For example, an embattled couple say they will miss their next appointment due to their annual camping trip, a distressed college student brightens up when she mentions talking to her aunt, or a recently immigrated mother comments that a woman next door invited her to a neighborhood festival. These seemingly mundane or tangential occurrences may reveal valuable resources that can be incorporated into solutions.

Asking about resources

In addition to listening and looking for resources, another simple way SBT practitioners uncover resources is by asking about them. This can be done with written or verbal strengths assessments at the beginning of, and throughout, therapeutic services. Persistent searches for strengths in clients' pasts, presents, and potential futures stand in sharp contrast with traditional problem-based assessments where resource assessments are either absent or rarely used to inform clinical work. Resource assessments that are integrated into treatment re-orient both the client *and* the counselor, helping them feel hopeful that change is possible. Clients become re-moralized as they begin to see themselves as capable of changing and leading more satisfying lives. As you consider the effect of the following questions, it is easy to see why resource-focused questions are generally more effective in engaging clients' hope, energy, and action.

- Problem-focused assessment questions:
    - What members of your family have suffered from depression?
    - What do you think are the roots of your problem?
- Resource-focused assessment questions:
    - When are times you have not been depressed?
    - How have you been able to manage, despite depression?
    - How have you been able to keep depression from ruining your day on some occasions?
    - Who in your family would not be surprised to see you get over this problem?
    - Who in your life can you enlist to work with you to deal with this problem?
    - Have you always been a fighter, or is this a new development?

Resource-based assessments also address family and cultural values, tapping into a wellspring of strengths:

- What values did you learn from your family about dealing with adversity?
- Who else in your life holds these values? How can you recruit them to stand with you against the problem?

Routine collection of client feedback also helps pinpoint resources. Figure 21.1 shows an example of the Outcome Rating Scale (ORS) from Better Outcomes Now (BON) (Duncan, 2017; https://betteroutcomesnow.com/#/) that was used in couples therapy. The scores are from one member of the couple, and indicate social resources (highest rating under the "Socially" domain) that can be explored for possible help in resolving problems in other domains.

Resource incorporation

The logical next step in recruiting client resources is engaging clients in explorations of whether their identified resources can be used to overcome problems and achieve goals, and how this could be done:

- For a client mourning the loss of loved ones and traditions from their home country, can a neighbor be an entry point into community connections that help alleviate the loneliness?
- Can a respected relative provide refuge for a young person whose parents struggle with addiction?
- How might a camping excursion provide clues for improving a couple's relationship?
- How does a cultural value of "staying strong" aid in an individual's fight against despair?

Answers to these types of questions unfold in therapeutic dialogue. Clients ultimately determine the meaning of these resources, and SBT clinicians affirm client meanings and collaborate with them on possible applications. This process not only reveals client resources, it *creates* change by treating clients as competent individuals capable of overcoming adversity and achieving goals that improve their lives.

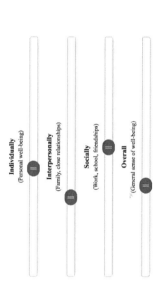

Figure 21.1 Example of completed Outcome Rating Scale (ORS) using Better Outcomes Now (BON) in couple therapy

Listening for change

Eric was dumbstruck when he learned that the couple he was seeing for the first time had not had sex in 10 years. This glaring fact somehow overshadowed everything else discussed in the session. For homework, Eric asked the couple to take note of times when they look at each other in the way they did in the early years of their marriage. The couple agreed and scheduled a next appointment.

Returning a week later, both members of the couple appeared markedly more upbeat. In fact, they looked at each other with sheepish grins, like co-conspirators in on a secret. As planned, Eric began by inquiring about their homework; they replied apologetically "We didn't really do that." Instead, they confessed they had had sex! Moreover, they were actually quite pleased with the experience! Eric smiled and nodded, then continued with his list of pre-planned questions.

Observing behind the one-way mirror, Eric's supervisor gasped —wait, wait, did he HEAR what they just said?! The supervisor quickly called Eric back and pointed out that the couple had just reported an epic change that needed to be discussed. He insisted Eric leave his carefully crafted notes and, instead, explore how this change happened and what it meant for their relationship. Baffled as to why he had not done this in the first place, Eric returned and, for the remainder of the session, invited the couple to give meaning to their news. Given they both agreed that it was a welcome change, he ended with asking them to consider what they might envision as a next step.

Developing a change mindset

It is easy to smile and chalk off this true story to trainee inexperience. But most deficit-focused psychotherapy is steeped in the belief that change will take time, especially for entrenched problems. The literature suggests otherwise; rapid change (within the first few sessions) and transformative change are not uncommon, even for longstanding difficulties (Bohart & Tallman, 2010). How therapists view change may actually inhibit it. The following assumptions, derived largely from solution-focused brief therapy (Berg, 1994) help realign beliefs to facilitate "hearing," responding to, and capitalizing on change:

- change is inevitable;
- all people are capable of change;
- small changes lead to larger changes;
- change in one part of a system leads to change in other parts of the system;
- a focus on change creates change;
- a focus on the future empowers change;
- talking about change makes it more likely to occur and be durable.

Embracing these assumptions creates a "change ear," a pre-requisite for hearing change.

Developing a "change ear"

In the above example, Eric missed a megaphone change announcement. However, in many instances, change is voiced with little fanfare. Listening with a change ear is like using a special hearing aid that magnifies any verbal or non-verbal communication about change. With practice, therapists can adjust the volume to perceive previously undetected change wavelengths. A kind look exchanged by a high-conflict couple or a shared giggle between a mother and her rebellious daughter can represent profound exceptions to presenting problems and potential avenues for transformative change.

Therapists attune their listening to any verbalization of change, no matter how understated. A mother with her highly-active 7-year-old might start a counseling session with "we had a pretty good week," but then launch into the assigned homework, tracking misbehavior. The mother and counselor settle into well-worn problem talk while the son disengages to play on the floor. A counselor with a honed change ear jumps in to ask mother and son to say more about the good week. After a thorough recap of the "good week," chances are the son becomes more present in the conversation. Alternatively, the therapist engages the mother in her preference to discuss misbehavior, while "good week" is etched either on a notepad or in mind, ready to bring forth at an opportune opening. Optimally, this happens sooner rather than later, allowing time to explore its meaning and potential as a solution, or the beginning of a solution.

Client feedback tools such as the Outcome Rating Scale (ORS) are stop-gap ways to detect change. Any score that is better, especially on the domain that represents the presenting concern, should jump out in sharp relief and lead to an inquiry of what it represents. Scores can either be small or large enough to constitute reliable change, such as 6 points or more on the ORS. Regardless, all change denoted warrants follow-up, typically early in the meeting.

Strategies for developing a change ear include the following:

- listen for client verbalizations of anything different;
- listen for client verbalizations of anything different related to the presenting problem;
- notice client behaviors that indicate change;
- notice client behaviors that indicate change related to the presenting problem;
- notice scores indicating change on a valid client feedback instrument;
- comment on any verbal, non-verbal, or client-scored progress instrument indicator of change;

- use expressions of surprise, leaning toward clients, or jotting change statements down on a notepad to punctuate client expressions of change;
- comment on noticed change as soon as possible;
- expand the meaning of the change from the client's perspective;
- inquire about the possibility of continuing changes into the future;
- assign homework that involves clients doing more of the activities they describe as indicative of change.

Not getting in the way

Discussing a child's misbehavior or why a marriage lacks intimacy assures clients that their therapist hears and understands their dilemma. But talking *only* about problems and overlooking "homegrown" solutions can block discovery of naturally occurring change. Without inviting clients to notice and expand functional aspects of their lives, therapists may inadvertently make problems more intractable. Listening for, hearing, punctuating, and amplifying change helps therapists not interfere with the natural tendency to survive and thrive. Therapists get out of clients' way by not allowing theories of dysfunction to select what is heard and deemed important in client narratives. This is perhaps the single most potent first step therapists can take to help clients move toward recovery and is an essential practical skill for any SBT clinician.

23

Asking resilience and coping questions

As Egan (2010) notes: "Like the rest of us, clients become what they talk about...so be careful about the questions you ask" (p. 292). In contrast to diagnostic questions about what is lacking or wrong with clients, strengths-based questions invite clients to acknowledge and capitalize on resources that can help them achieve their goals. This chapter describes and illustrates one of the most commonly used types of questions in SBT—questions aimed at discovering, detailing, and applying clients' ever-present resilience and coping skills.

Every client is resilient

The term *resilience* originated in the physical sciences to describe the ability of an object, like a spring, to retain its original form after being stretched. When applied to people, resilience entails much more than simply bouncing back. Human resilience involves a dynamic interplay of personal and social factors that help a person cope, survive, or even thrive in the face of adverse circumstances.

While people differ in their level of resilience, *everyone* is resilient because life is challenging regardless of one's circumstances. Therefore, counselors can be sure that every individual, couple, or family sitting in front of them offers a one-of-a-kind set of resilience and coping skills. The following questions help SBT clinicians explore such skills:

- With everything going on in your life, how do you manage to get up each day and take care of business?

- What keeps you from giving up?
- Where do you find the courage to face these challenges?
- How have you kept things from getting worse?
- What would your friends say they most appreciate about the way you've handled this challenge?

The above questions clarify clients' resiliency and convey faith in their ability to stand up to life's difficulties. The following story illustrates the use of resilience and coping questions with a young client who displayed a remarkable ability to bend, but not break, under very challenging conditions.

Shay's story

Shay, age 18, entered therapy at the request of the school counselor. Her grades were rapidly declining, she was skipping school, and she told the school counselor that she was "tired and burnt out." The referral form depicted Shay as "a bright student" capable of succeeding at school when she applied herself.

Shay's resilience was obvious. Her father left home when she was six months old, never to be heard from again. She experienced physical and sexual abuse, lived in four foster homes, and had attended six different schools since the age of five. Shay told the counselor no one wanted her and family members treated her like an inconvenience. She worked the midnight-to-morning shift at a local cafe to support herself and her mother.

A good part of the first session involved hearing and validating Shay's fatigue and frustration with the daily grind of work and school. The counselor asked how she managed to keep the counseling appointment amidst her many obligations. Shay said her recent meeting with the school counselor made her realize how bad things had become at school. When asked about her best hopes for life, she expressed a desire to attend college and have a family of her own someday. The following exchange took place early in the second session.

Counselor: With everything you've been through, what keeps you from giving up?

Shay: If I was going to give up, I would have done it long ago. But I'm old enough now to do things on my own instead of relying on my mom or family for money. I'm not saying everything's great, but I've made it this far so why stop now?

Counselor: That's my question. You've gone through things that would make it easy to lose hope and give up. But here you are, still standing, moving along, thinking about going to college. How do you do it?

Shay: I just do. I know I have problems and I've had it worse than most kids. I'm used to it. I've had to handle a lot of things.

Counselor: You sure have.

Shay: But nothing goes on forever, even though it feels that way when you're in it.

Counselor: What do you mean?

Shay: When things get bad, I tell myself it won't last forever.

Counselor: Ah, okay. So reminding yourself that bad times don't last forever helps you get through those times?

Shay: Yes. But I wasn't always like that. I thought about ending it all when I was 15. Things were terrible at home and I wanted to quit school.

Counselor: How are you different now compared to then?

Shay described additional actions and attributes that helped her cope with adversity, such as writing poetry, taking walks, talking with trusted friends, and a desire to "be somebody." The counselor and Shay explored how she could adapt and apply these self-styled coping strategies toward her hopes of attending college and having a family of her own. Despite ongoing challenges at home and school, as well as a few unexpected setbacks, Shay graduated from high school and made plans to attend a local community college.

As illustrated with Shay, asking resilience and coping questions in SBT does not ignore or minimize the significant impact of poverty, child abuse, or other hardships. In the midst of these challenges, however, clients are *always* doing something to help themselves manage and cope. In other words, they are being resilient. SBT helps clients apply their one-of-a-kind resilience and coping skills toward their hopes and goals.

24

Building on exceptions

In addition to hearing and validating clients' concerns and problems, SBT clinicians are curious about "the better times" when problems are absent or less noticeable in clients' lives. These occasions of strength and success—called "exceptions to the problem" in solution-focused therapy (de Shazer et al., 2007)—can serve as important building blocks to change. The process of building on exceptions in SBT involves three steps—eliciting, exploring, and expanding.

Eliciting

SBT practitioners can elicit or discover exceptions by looking, listening, and asking for them.

Looking. Looking for exceptions in reports and other documents may reveal what clients are already doing to help themselves before they even get to counseling. For example, in reviewing the chart of an adolescent client (Jane) hospitalized for frequent aggressive behavior, the SBT clinician might notice that Jane had significantly fewer aggression infractions following recreation activities compared to other times of the day. These post-recreation times represent important exceptions to the aggression problem. SBT clinicians also look for exceptions in therapy sessions. For example, a polite exchange between a quarrelsome husband and wife during a therapy session represents an exception to their arguing problem.

Listening. Listening to what clients say and how they say it provides another way to identify exceptions. The ongoing experience of a problem makes it hard to notice small but significant fluctuations in its presence and intensity, which is why SBT practitioners listen for any hints of exceptions when meeting with clients. The italicized words and phrases in the following client statements provide clues about exceptions: I'm depressed *almost* constantly; I hate everything about school *except* science; My wife and I *rarely* talk about anything important anymore. In the first example, "almost" suggests there are times when depression is absent or less intense. Similarly, the word "rarely" in the last example implies the couple discusses important matters, though not as much as desired.

Asking. Inquiring about exceptions in SBT may involve questions, tasks, or rating scales. Exception-seeking questions include the following: When is depression less noticeable?; What times of the school day are a little more tolerable?; When was the last time you and your wife had an important conversation and what did you discuss? As with other SBT techniques, these questions should never be forced on clients and should always be done with careful attention to their preferences and perceptions. For example, direct questions work well for certain clients ("When doesn't the problem happen in your family?"), whereas other clients prefer indirect questions that explicitly acknowledge and accommodate their perceptions ("I appreciate your honesty in saying your relationship with your parents sucks. I'm curious when things suck a little less between you and your parents?").

SBT clinicians also use the following types of tasks to elicit exceptions:

- For the next two days, pay attention to times when the problem doesn't happen and list what you or others did differently during those times.
- Between now and next week's meeting, observe anything about your husband you don't want to change.

In addition to questions and tasks, rating scales offer another means for discovering exceptions. Even though most scales focus on client deficits, SBT clinicians can discover exceptions in items scored as less problematic than others.

BUILDING ON EXCEPTIONS

Exploring

Once exceptions are identified, the following questions explore exception-related details and circumstances: What did you do differently to make it (the exception) happen?; What was different about the time you and your wife had a good conversation? How would you explain the fact that things went better between you and your parents last week?

The next exchange took place during a meeting with Anthony, a 15-year-old who was recently suspended from school for disruptive and aggressive classroom behavior. The conversation picks up just after the therapist discovered that Anthony exhibited considerably fewer behavior problems in math as compared to his other classes.

Therapist: How would you explain your success in math class, Anthony?

Anthony: [*shrugs shoulders*] I don't know.

Therapist: How is math class different for you than your other classes?

Anthony: I don't know. I like the teacher, usually. She's funnier than my other teachers.

Therapist: Okay. What else is different about her or the class compared to your other classes?

Anthony: She acts like a real person, not a prison guard or something.

Therapist: Interesting. What does she do or say that's more like a real person?

Anthony: She jokes around with us a little and doesn't take everything so seriously. Sometimes she'll talk to me about music and things I'm actually interested in. My other teachers don't do that. They're all business. They don't care about what we like or what we do outside of school.

Therapist: And how does all this affect you and your behavior in her class?

Anthony: I treat her better because she treats me better.

Therapist: That makes sense. What else about math class, or your approach to it, might help to explain your success in that class compared to your other classes?

Anthony: I sit closer to the front, but I'm not sure that has anything to do with it.

As the therapist explored additional details of the "math class exception" and other exceptions at school, it became clear that Anthony was capable of behaving successfully with teachers he did not like. As seen with Anthony, SBT clinicians explore exceptions with the same analytic rigor and scrutiny commonly applied to exploring problems. Although both types of information are useful, clients often become more engaged and energized when discussing exceptions—perhaps because these discussions are so different from the more typical, problem-driven conversations clients have with themselves and helping professionals. In addition to engaging clients' attention and hope, exploring exceptions lays the foundation for the third step of building on exceptions in SBT.

Expanding

Using information about the details and circumstances of exceptions, SBT clinicians encourage clients to do more of what is already working. This encouragement may take the form of an experiment. For example, Anthony's therapist invited him to apply his math class (exception) behavior to another class for one week and observe any changes that result from it. Similarly, after learning that Anthony sat toward the front of the room in math class and that the teacher occasionally joked with students and asked about their interests, the therapist encouraged other teachers to consider these strategies in their interactions with Anthony.

Building on exceptions is based on the fact that change is constant, and every problem—no matter how constant it may seem—fluctuates in frequency and intensity. Unfortunately, serious problems often monopolize the attention of clients and therapists, making it hard to notice the brighter moments of life. Like diamonds in the rough, exceptions typically fall under the radar and remain unnoticed unless SBT clinicians actively seek them out. As with other SBT techniques, the strategy of building on exceptions is collaboratively selected and implemented with careful attention to the client's preferences and feedback.

25

Co-creating new stories

SBT assumes all clients offer strengths and resources that can help them make desired changes. However, these assets are often concealed by prevalent one-dimensional stories of defeat and deficit held by clients. The longer these stories persist, the harder it is for clients to view themselves as separate from their struggles. When clients see themselves through the narrow lens of "having" or "being" a problem—a view often reinforced by mental health professions—it is difficult for them to generate the hope and resources needed to support new stories.

SBT offers many techniques to help clients create more hopeful, multi-storied accounts of their lives. Examples include listening for change, asking about resilience, and recruiting client resources. This chapter borrows from narrative approaches to offer another way in which SBT clinicians collaborate with clients to co-create preferred stories and self-identities.

Conducting externalizing conversations

Based on the motto, "the person is not the problem—the problem is the problem," White and Epston (1990) began conducting externalizing conversations (hereafter "externalizing") to help clients view problems as external to and separate from themselves. Externalizing is not a one-time intervention, but an ongoing conversational process that helps clients switch from an internalized perception of having or being a problem ("I have depression"; "I am bipolar") to an externalized perception of being *in a relationship with the problem* ("When did you and Depression first meet?"). Fusing one's identity with one's struggles limits possibilities of change and growth.

SBT clinicians conduct externalizing conversations that invite clients to realign their relationship with problems and create new stories or "counter-narratives" of competency and ingenuity. Regardless of the problem's dominant description—depression, anxiety, ADHD, etc.—externalizing portrays it as peripheral to clients' identity and merely one of many possible client-related stories. More specifically, SBT views psychiatric diagnoses and other totalizing, deficit-based descriptions as narrow misrepresentations of the complexities and possibilities of clients.

In keeping with the client-directed and alliance-minded foundations of SBT, externalizing conversations are not imposed on clients by therapists. Rather, they are introduced in an invitational manner that gives clients full freedom to accept or reject them.

Meeting clients apart from the problem. Externalizing begins by meeting the person apart from the problem through questions such as "What do you like doing for fun?" and "What is your idea of a good weekend?" Once SBT clinicians get to know who the client is as a person, they "meet the problem" by asking questions like "When did you first meet the problem?" and "How has your relationship with it changed over time?" Inviting clients to name the problem (Depression, Meany, etc.) facilitates the externalizing process.

Asking relative influence questions. Having met the person and problem as described above, SBT therapists ask *relative influence questions* to clarify the problem's influence on the person (problem-influence questions) and the person's influence on the problem (person-influence questions). For example, the following *problem-influence questions* explore how the problem has affected clients and key persons:

- How has depression affected you physically?
- How does depression influence your relationships with your family? Your partner/spouse? Your children?
- How does depression impact your work life?
- What tricks has depression used to control you?

Some clients become more energized when they describe the problem's influence. Elise, a high-achieving adolescent, entered counseling with a diagnosis of depression, a medication prescription, and the burdensome belief that she was destined to a life of depression similar to that of her grandmother. She appeared distant at first, but became more emotional and engaged when asked how depression affected her physically, socially, and other ways. She tearfully described the problem's adverse effect on her energy level, self-confidence, and relationships with family and friends. She described how depression had prevented her from engaging in previously enjoyable activities like hiking and being with friends. As the conversation evolved, Elise became increasingly intrigued by the idea of being in a relationship with depression rather than "having" depression.

SBT clinicians follow up problem-influence conversations with *person-influence questions* such as the following ones used with Elise:

- Tell me about a time you kept depression from dominating a situation. How did you do that?
- You said you felt more "in control" and "connected" when working at the restaurant. How do you resist depression's urgings at work?
- What strategies help you stand up to depression rather than yielding to its demands?

Person-influence questions often reveal unacknowledged and unappreciated client abilities. Amplifying these competencies helps strengthen the new counter-story and deconstruct the deficit-based story. For example, as Elise described strategies that counteracted the problem's influence and supported the evolving story of courage and competency, the narrower story of weakness and deficiency played a less prominent role in her self-identity and actions.

Externalizing metaphors. SBT practitioners use the following types of metaphors to facilitate clients' participation in externalizing conversations: Standing up to the problem, resisting the problem's

DISTINCTIVE PRACTICAL FEATURES OF SBT

demands, declining the problem's invitations, taking a sabbatical from the problem, writing one's own script rather than following the problem's script, and dancing to one's own tune rather than the problem's music. These and other metaphors are not canned or pre-planned, but are developed or chosen to fit each client's situation and style. For example, Elise responded to the themes of "standing up" to depression and "reclaiming" her life, which enhanced her growing realization that she could write her own story rather than capitulating to depression.

Sustaining the new story

Once clients begin to embrace and enact the new story, SBT clinicians use various techniques to help them sustain the story and corresponding actions. Two such methods are described below.

Recruiting social support. SBT practitioners collaborate with clients to recruit people who can help clients sustain positive changes that accompany the new story. For example, the clinician asked Elise, "Of everyone you know, who would support your effort to reclaim your life from depression?" Elise named 23 people in a matter of minutes! The clinician and Elise discussed specific strategies for recruiting "Team Elise" and enlisting the support from team members when needed.

Treating clients as consultants. Another way SBT clinicians help clients sustain new stories is by inviting clients to serve as consultants. This technique is illustrated by the following questions for Elise:

- My job is helping people change their relationship with problems as you've done. If you were a counselor, how would you go about helping others do that?
- Since you've demonstrated expertise in making changes, what advice would you offer a friend hoping to make similar changes?
- Would you be willing to share your wisdom with me and others by making a list of everything that has helped you make these changes?

- A lot of people could benefit from your experience and wisdom, so I'm wondering if you'd be willing to write a story about your journey. If so, could I share your story with others?

In addition to discussing these questions, the clinician invited Elise to join a Consultant Club consisting of children and adolescents who had made successful changes and were willing to share their wisdom with the clinician and others in the future (Murphy, 2015). Elise accepted the invitation.

As White (2007) observed: "Many people who seek therapy believe that the problems of their lives are a reflection of their own identity" and "this belief only sinks them further into the problems they are attempting to resolve" (p. 9). Externalizing offers a competing perspective that empowers clients to rewrite their life stories in ways that align with their hopes, strengths, and values.

26

Using between-session strategies

Since SBT trusts clients to adapt and apply therapy content in ways that fit their unique styles and circumstances, therapist-directed "homework assignments" are not a routine part of strengths-based practice. However, there are times when SBT clinicians use between-session activities that emerge naturally from therapeutic conversations and client goals. In keeping with the collaborative tone of SBT, these activities are (a) *suggested* rather than imposed ("What would you think about ...?"), and (b) *situated* in the therapist's curiosity and the client's own words, hopes, and goals ("Since you want to improve things between you and your daughter, what would you think about making a note of the times the two of you get along better during the coming week?"). With these points in mind, between-session activities can be helpful in sustaining therapeutic conversations from one session to the next, amplifying key therapeutic themes and ideas, and encouraging clients to put therapeutic conversations into action in their everyday lives.

Every client and conversation is unique, which means there is an unlimited number of potential between-session strategies in SBT. Four such strategies are described below.

Letters

People generally like to receive letters, especially those that do not require a payment. SBT practitioners periodically write between-session letters to clients for various reasons—to reinforce in-session themes that resonate with clients, to highlight clients' hopes and preferred stories, to invite experimentation with new ideas or actions, and to empower clients' progress toward therapeutic goals. These elements, along with other aspects of SBT noted in italics, are illustrated below in a letter to Elise from Chapter 25. The letter was sent a few days after her third therapy session, during which she reported marked progress on her goal of improving her relationship with family and friends.

> Dear Elise,
>
> Congratulations on your recent efforts to improve things between you and your family and friends *(acknowledging progress and addressing key themes and goals of therapy)*. It takes courage and determination to do what you have done *(complimenting and giving credit)*. I would love to find out how you did it *(expressing curiosity)* so that I could share your wisdom with others *(advising others)*, if that's okay with you *(asking permission)*. I look forward to our next visit.

Writing letters on paper or electronic media takes time. It is impractical for clinicians to write to every client or between every session. However, clients have reported that a short letter can make a big difference (Bjorøy, Madigan, & Nylund, 2015), which is why between-session letters are a staple in the SBT toolbox.

Gentle encouragement

SBT assumes clients possess the wisdom and abilities needed to improve their lives. Thus, therapy is often a matter of helping them access and apply existing resources toward therapeutic goals. Sometimes clients just need a little encouragement to implement ideas or actions they've considered but haven't yet applied in their everyday lives. Here are a few examples of how SBT clinicians gently encourage clients to put their ideas, hopes, and resources into action between sessions:

- You mentioned how important it is for you to be the kind of loving parent you never had as a child. Would you be willing

to think about or even try out something this week to get you closer to the parent you want to be?
- When you said how much you respect your grandparents, it made me wonder what they might say or do to help you out. How possible is it for you to contact them during the coming week to get their take on things?
- When I asked what you wanted from therapy, you said you wanted to start a new chapter of life that was very different from previous chapters—especially in situations involving conflicts with loved ones. I'm wondering what would happen if you tried something very different from your usual response the next time a potential conflict starts to occur. What do you think?

Observation tasks

Observation tasks invite clients to observe specific between-session experiences related to therapeutic goals and conversations. For example, SBT clinicians can invite clients to observe any events or experiences that enhance their therapeutic goals *regardless* of what those goals are. The adaptability of observation tasks to various clients and various goals makes them particularly well-suited to the client-directed nature of SBT. The following example illustrates an observation task used with Isaac, an adolescent client who told the clinician he was "in a slump" and wanted to "get back on track" with his family and school work:

> It's been a really tough month for you, Isaac. I definitely can see why you're so concerned *(appreciation and validation)*. Since you want to break this slump and get back on track with your family and school work *(situating the observation task in Isaac's comments and goals)*, it might be helpful to be on the lookout this week for anything you or others do that helps improve things at school or with your family. You could even make a list of these things and we can review the list when we meet next week. What do you think?

Asking Isaac to document his observations in the form of a list leads to the next strategy.

Lists

Making lists is a common activity for many people, whether it be grocery lists or daily "to do" lists. SBT clinicians can incorporate people's natural tendency to make lists into between-session tasks that emerge directly from therapeutic conversations and address the client's hopes, goals, and resources:

- You've already mentioned a few people who care about you, and I'm wondering if you could make a list of every person in your life who cares and wants the best for you. If you're willing to do that, then we can review the list at our next meeting and discuss how you might go about recruiting help and support for your goal of becoming a better father to your kids. How does that sound to you?
- You came here to improve your relationship with your daughter, so I wanted to ask if you're willing to make a list of the times when you get along well—or a little better than usual—during the coming week. Your list might give us clues about how to increase the better times and improve the relationship. What do you think?
- Since you know your situation better than anyone else, would you be willing to make a list of anything you can think of that might help you turn things around?

The strategies in this chapter serve to "keep the conversation going" between sessions and to assist clients in putting their theories, strengths, goals, and other resources into action.

Collecting systematic client feedback

SBT holds that collaborative partnerships harness the innate knowledge and resourcefulness of clients. Creating a continuous loop of client feedback is one of the most important ways SBT clinicians collaborate with clients. This process is dialogical, meaning the therapist and client listen to, engage with, and are informed by each other's ideas. This differs from traditional practices based on preconceived notions of what is wrong with clients and what they need, monologues derived from theories and codified assessments. SBT insists that clients' views and their incorporation into therapy are the keys to success.

SBT's emphasis on client feedback shapes all counseling conversations. Counselors can propose novel ideas and new ways to view and resolve client dilemmas, but clients have the final say in accepting, rejecting, or modifying them. Clients determine the relevance of therapist input, adding their own embellishments to create new understandings and pathways to change.

Systematic client feedback (SCF) has gained increasing prominence in psychotherapies seeking to improve outcomes and provide valid outcome data (Sparks & Duncan, in press). SCF uses valid and reliable instruments to ascertain client perceptions of the alliance or lack of progress, and to immediately address any concerns before they lead to negative outcomes. One SCF system, the Partners for Change Outcome Management System (PCOMS; Duncan & Reese, 2015), uniquely operationalizes SBT's collaborative values.

PCOMS implementation

PCOMS' measures include two valid and reliable progress instruments—the Outcome Rating Scale (ORS; ages 13 and over; Miller

& Duncan, 2000) and Child Outcome Rating Scale (CORS; ages 6–12; Duncan, Miller, & Sparks, 2003a)—and two alliance measures, the Session Rating Scale (SRS; ages 13 and over; Miller, Duncan, & Johnson, 2002) and the Child Session Rating Scale (CSRS; ages 6–12; Duncan, Miller, & Sparks, 2003b). These measures are displayed in Appendix A.

Progress ratings are collected at the beginning of every session using the ORS, and alliance ratings are collected at the end using the SRS. Clients indicate their views by placing a mark on each of the four lines or moving a dot on an iPad or other tablet device, and scoring is done via paper and pencil or iPads/tablets linked to a web-based system such as Better Outcomes Now (BON) (Duncan, 2017; https://betteroutcomesnow.com/#/). For web-based applications, clients touch and move small circles on a screen; this automatically displays graphs of clients' scores in relation to clinical cutoffs, expected treatment response (ETR), and clients' treatment trajectories compared with the ETR (see Figure 27.1).

Customized dashboards give alerts for at-risk clients and provide an array of reports at clinician, program, and agency levels. In addition, PCOMS has been adapted for use with couples and families (Sparks & Duncan, 2018). The process helps highlight the diversity of perspectives common in systemic practice.

Scoring and discussion of client ratings generally require as little as 3 minutes, allowing routine use in everyday practice. The meaning of client ratings is then explored through therapist questioning and ensuing dialogue. Thus, scores represent both valid indications of client status and unique stories that can only be discovered conversationally. This process facilitates counselors' understanding of clients' specific circumstances and enhances the fit of services.

PCOMS as a dialogical tool

For many clinicians, numbers and graphs may seem counterproductive to quality clinical process. PCOMS was developed as a tool that would not disrupt the conversational flow between clients and

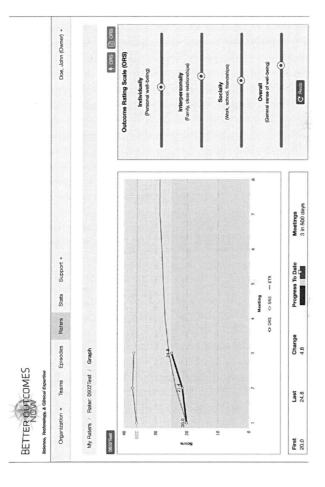

Figure 27.1 Better Outcomes Now (BON) graph with client's ORS scores (thick bottom line) and expected treatment response (ETR) (long middle line). Progress meter shows client to be less than 50% of ETR, suggesting a client/counselor conversation about changing therapeutic directions

counselors crucial for alliance formation and client engagement. The goal is to *enhance* therapist/client collaboration through mutual exploration of problems, goals, and solutions (Sparks & Duncan, 2018). PCOMS was created to be: 1) feasible for everyday use; 2) transparently shared; and 3) grounded in client, not theoretical, descriptions. Administering and scoring the instruments is just the beginning, as it opens avenues for exploring client meanings, ideas, and hopes for the future. The following conversation illustrates Ben's use of the ORS with a client (Anna) struggling with depression:

Ben: [*showing Anna the instrument*] I like to use this instrument with clients at each meeting. It tells me your view of how you are doing. This way, we know if things are getting better and, if not, we can talk about doing something different. Would you be willing to do that?

Anna: Sure. Okay.

Ben: Great. If you could just put a mark on each of these four lines that lets me know how you are doing in each of these areas. Marks on the right mean things are going pretty well, and marks toward the left mean not so good.

Anna: [*scores ORS*]

Ben: [*after tabulating her score on the ORS*] So your total score is 21. For this instrument, there is something called a cutoff, which is 25. Your score is just below that, meaning you fall into the category of people who enter counseling and seek something different in their life. Does that fit for you?

Anna: Yeah.

Ben: Okay, so this will kind of be an anchor point for us, to let us know if what we're doing here is helping or not. I notice that your lowest score is on the interpersonal scale. Is that what you're here about?

Anna: Yes. I just went through a bad divorce.

Ben: Okay. Do you want to start with that, or somewhere else?

The conversation above is a snapshot of PCOMS in action. Notice that Ben always asks Anna if what he presumes from the scores is accurate. The client can confirm or disconfirm, and then relate her story. The tool never *is* the truth, but is only a vehicle for entering clients' idiosyncratic truths and meanings. Thus, PCOMS is a dialogical/communicative tool that goes well beyond simply measuring change. At the same time, PCOMS conforms to core SBT principles by:

- ensuring that client content forms the basis and direction of therapeutic dialogue;
- offering a methodology for creating authentic, client-directed therapeutic partnerships;
- helping level the therapeutic hierarchy by privileging clients' perspectives;
- providing a clinical tool for learning about and incorporating client perspectives, values, cultural influences, and ideas about change;
- fostering client engagement and strengthening the therapeutic alliance.

28

Creating strengths-based work environments

Most behavioral healthcare practitioners have been exposed to training in client strengths and may use inventories that ask about client resources. Despite this, the culture of many settings is problem-based, reflecting the amplification of client deficit via diagnosis and theories of pathology. Deficit-based assumptions structure typical mental health procedures and shape how practitioners discuss, write about, and interact with clients. Becoming strengths based requires a deliberate overhaul of many taken-for-granted aspects of the service environment. Without this, even an ardent commitment to a strengths-based perspective can falter.

Assessing the environment

Assessment is the first step in creating strengths-based work environments. This is done by systematically matching the realities of day-to-day practice with SBT principles. A simple grid facilitates this process, with SBT values on one side and the site's adherence to such values on the other. Once the grid is completed, strengths and weaknesses related to SBT are clearly visible. From this starting point, specific goals and steps can be devised to more fully align the site with SBT.

Key principles to include on the y axis (vertical) are:

- Collaboration—elements that invite client participation and engagement.
- Respect—elements that communicate respect for client strengths and dignity.

DISTINCTIVE PRACTICAL FEATURES OF SBT

- Warmth/Friendliness—elements that treat clients as guests and enhance their comfort.
- Flexibility—elements that honor client uniqueness.

The x axis (horizontal) would include:

- Space—arrangement of the site's physical environment and website.
- Procedures—intake, scheduling, staff meetings, data protocols, etc.
- Paperwork—progress notes, closing reports, case summaries, payment forms, etc.
- Language—spoken and written language used to communicate with or about clients.

Though other dimensions can be added, the SBT Site Assessment Grid might look like Figure 28.1.

SITE NAME:			DATE:	
	SPACE	PROCEDURES	PAPERWORK	LANGUAGE
COLLABORATION				
RESPECT				
WARMTH/ FRIENDLINESS				
FLEXIBILITY				

Figure 28.1 Example of SBT Site Assessment Grid

The above grid can be used by administrators and clinicians, in small or large groups, at routine staff meetings, or at monthly, bi-monthly, or yearly retreats. Using it regularly helps pinpoint deficit-based practices and provides a foundation for targeted change.

Matching SBT values to practice

Each area of the SBT Site Assessment Grid can lead to specific plans for change. The following discussion describes potential strategies practice sites might adopt to align more fully with SBT.

Space. The physical environment includes waiting areas, offices, counseling and conference rooms, and virtual spaces. Clients' first impressions of these elements can profoundly impact their experience of being valued or devalued. Clean, comfortable seating in a well-lit, peacefully decorated waiting room (with a dedicated space for meaningful play activities for children when they are part of the client base) lets clients know that they matter (Respect). Easy access to someone at the front desk (not behind a glass window) communicates that staff are there for clients and want them to feel comfortable (Warmth/Friendliness; Collaboration). This category also includes the following environmental considerations and accommodations:

- Access to and use of outdoor spaces to encourage particular clients to engage and participate (e.g., a table tennis room or basketball court for young persons).
- Meeting clients in alternate locations such as homes, schools, or community centers shows clients a willingness to accommodate their preferences and enhance their comfort (Collaboration; Flexibility).

Procedures. These are day-to-day practices that align with SBT.

- Communicating clearly (phone calls, brochures, mailings, website information, etc.) about procedures invites client engagement (Collaboration).

- Describing how and why client feedback is routinely collected assures clients that their voice is critical for effective counseling (Collaboration; Respect; Flexibility).
- Tailoring procedures to client preferences indicates that therapeutic services are truly aimed at working towards what is best for the client (Collaboration; Respect; Flexibility).
- Privileging client perspectives in assessments and treatment plans ensures collaborative, client-directed services (Collaboration; Respect; Flexibility).
- Structuring staff meetings around client feedback data actualizes client input, even when clients cannot be physically present (Collaboration; Respect; Flexibility).
- Inviting clients to devise questions for team meetings, recording meetings where clients are discussed and sharing these recordings with clients, or routinely consulting with clients on the focus of progress notes all serve to prioritize client preferences and involvement (Collaboration; Respect; Flexibility).
- Providing clients with counselors who speak the client's first language when possible indicates the desire to maximize client engagement and input (Collaboration; Respect; Flexibility).

Paperwork. Translating forms into languages spoken by clients and using gender-inclusive and "people first" language in paperwork and conversations communicates that the site is welcoming and inclusive (Collaboration; Respect; Warmth/Friendliness; Flexibility). Assessment and goal forms include ample space for clients' descriptions of their views and preferences as well as clients' strengths (Collaboration). Goal forms connect client strengths with change strategies (Collaboration; Flexibility).

Language. Reduce or eliminate medical and psychological jargon that does not conform to client descriptions (Collaboration; Respect; Flexibility). In settings where payment structures prohibit this, make a concerted effort to put client descriptions and language at the fore-front of paperwork and conversation (Collaboration; Respect; Flexibility). Working on a "down-in-the-dumps" problem rather than "depression" privileges clients' language and promotes client-driven options for change. SBT therapists refrain from translating client talk into professional idioms that restrict recovery and eschew client understandings. SBT language and paperwork fuels, and is fueled by, client descriptions and language. Thus, SBT paperwork engenders thoughts and actions that put clients' expertise front and center in devising treatment strategies.

Tailoring SBT to unique work sites

Just as each client is unique, so is each practice site. The above suggestions are general starting points. There are countless other strategies for transforming work environments to support SBT (e.g., see Duncan & Sparks, 2010). The process can start with questions from a staff member or from the inspiration of a senior administrator. Tools such as the SBT Site Assessment Grid can facilitate creative discussions and site-specific plans. The crucial starting point is a genuine desire to arrange the environment in ways that honor clients' inherent strengths and pivotal roles. Fewer dropouts and better outcomes are but two of the many possible benefits of creating strengths-based work environments that welcome and maximize client participation.

29

Integrating SBT into training and supervision

SBT practitioners are cultivated by SBT-dedicated training and supportive supervisory relationships. This chapter describes characteristics of training and supervisory environments that nurture SBT practices for trainees and seasoned professionals alike.

SBT graduate training

Ideally, trainees are taught SBT principles from the very beginning through the end of their graduate studies. In reality, training more likely falls somewhere along a continuum, with optimal at one end and business-as-usual at the other. Optimal entails continuous integration of SBT as a transtheoretical approach throughout a student's program while business-as-usual includes an SBT reference or teaching module here or there. In business-as-usual training programs, students may learn what a strengths-based perspective is but not know how to implement it in real-world practice.

The following are guidelines for educators who want to create optimal learning environments that produce skilled SBT practitioners.

- Discuss adoption of a strengths-based perspective with colleagues as a core foundation for curriculum development.
- Regularly review your training program's success at incorporating strengths-based principles, and strategize on ways to increase integration in all coursework and clinical training.
- Start all pre-practice courses with modules focused on common factors and strengths-based values.

- Ask trainees observing or listening to therapy sessions to identify and comment on clients' and counselors' strengths.
- During student role-plays, comment on what clients and therapists do well and ask observing students to do likewise.
- Include critical, empirically-driven perspectives in readings, lectures, and exercises when teaching deficit-focused diagnostic assessments and procedures.
- Use language in ways that cast clients as resourceful heroes and essential contributors to effective therapy.
- Help students identify social/contextual factors that create or constrain solutions to client concerns (e.g., routine use of eco-maps for assessment and goal setting).
- Use hands-on exercises to build trainees' skills in listening for, eliciting, and incorporating client strengths.
- Teach systematic client feedback from pre-practice through advance practice courses.
- Focus on client and student strengths in supervision.
- Cultivate an appreciation of a strengths-based perspective among community stakeholders, especially at practicum and internship sites.

Educators and trainers can adapt and expand these, or develop others, to fit the unique goals of their programs.

Post-graduate training in SBT

In many instances, practitioners become acquainted with SBT well beyond their formal schooling. Whether by attending a workshop on SBT, picking up a book at a conference, or stumbling upon a website, professionals may become inspired to incorporate SBT practices into their work. The following resources can help advanced practitioners expand their knowledge of SBT and become part of a broader SBT community:

- http://strengths.gallup.com/default.aspx
- www.heartandsoulofchange.com/

- www.sfbta.org/Default.aspx
- http://dulwichcentre.com.au/what-is-narrative-therapy/
- www.pluralistictherapy.com/
- *On Becoming a Better Therapist: Evidence-Based Practice One Client at a Time*, 2nd edition, by Barry L. Duncan, American Psychological Association.
- The *Handbook of Pluralistic Counselling and Psychotherapy*, edited by Mick Cooper and Wendy Dryden, Sage Publications.
- *The Strengths Perspective in Social Work Practice*, 6th edition, by Dennis Saleebey, Pearson Education.

SBT supervision

The language and focus of supervision inevitably gets replicated in therapy. A strengths-based approach begins in and is maintained by the supervisory conversation, where SBT supervisors and supervisees generate ways to actualize the belief that all clients have strengths. SBT supervisors also seek to mobilize supervisee strengths. Empowered supervisees bring renewed energy and optimism into their work with clients. Supervisors' positive regard for clients *and* supervisees ultimately enlivens the counseling process and helps create productive supervisory and therapeutic relationships.

Three primary skills underpin SBT supervision:

1. centering client voice in the supervisory process;
2. engaging supervisees in strengths-based discussions about clients;
3. highlighting and utilizing supervisees' talents and strengths.

Centering client voice. To center clients' views, SBT supervisors routinely inquire about the following:

- What does the client want to achieve?
- What type of service does the client think would be most helpful?
- How do clients feel about the therapy relationship?

Focusing on these key alliance components is a way to contextualize the stories supervisees tell about the therapy. They aid in "taking a step back" and reorienting the discussion around client goals and concerns.

Supervisors may not always be able to discern clients' actual viewpoints in supervisees' responses to the above questions. They then can request that supervisees select sections of audio or video recordings that support their descriptions of clients' perspectives. A more direct way to ensure that clients' views guide supervisory discussions is to require supervisees to collect systematic client feedback (SCF). SCF data helps to focus supervision on the meaning of client scores on feedback instruments, to identify clients at risk for negative outcomes, and to ensure that clients' views become the basis for adjusting, or generating new, therapy directions. Ultimately, clients are the final arbiters of what their scores mean. Supervisors can request that supervisees confirm with clients any hypotheses or strategies developed during supervision.

SCF systems that use web-based applications help center supervision around clients who need it most. For example, Better Outcomes Now (Duncan, 2017; https://betteroutcomesnow.com/#/) provides snapshots of clients not progressing as expected and at risk of dropping out. Figure 29.1 shows a hypothetical caseload that supervisors and supervisees can review prior to and during supervision. Arrows pointing to the left under "Progress to Date" indicate at-risk clients who are not progressing as expected.

Figure 29.2 depicts the client's expected treatment response (ETR), another tool for determining clients' progress status. The client's view of progress (thick bottom line representing ORS scores) is dipping below the ETR (long middle line). This signals the need for an immediate discussion with the client about what can be done to redirect the line upward. Knowing this prior to supervision facilitates brainstorming new directions to present to the client for consideration. The top line (SRS scores) represents the client's view of the therapy relationship, which is invaluable in identifying and addressing emerging alliance ruptures that may contribute to lack of progress.

My Rater

Rater	Service	First	Last (Date)	Change	Meetings	Progress To Date	Actions
0210		24.0	19.2 (2017-11-28)	-4.8	11		
0411		18.6	31.6 (2017-10-17)	13.0	5		
0526		19.4	23.4 (2017-10-19)	4.0	3		
0601-1		17.1	18.5 (2016-06-01)	1.4	2		
0601-CR-1		8.3	26.1 (2017-01-12)	17.8	3		
0601-CR-2		12.3	12.3 (2017-12-15)	0.0	1	‹ 2 Meetings	
0602Test		20.0	24.8 (2017-10-17)	4.8	3		
0607		13.7	17.8 (2016-06-08)	4.1	2		
0608		18.6	20.5 (2016-06-08)	1.9	2		
0622		15.3	24.8 (2016-06-24)	9.5	2		

Figure 29.1 Better Outcomes Now (BON) rater page depicting at-risk clients (i.e., clients with arrows to the left)

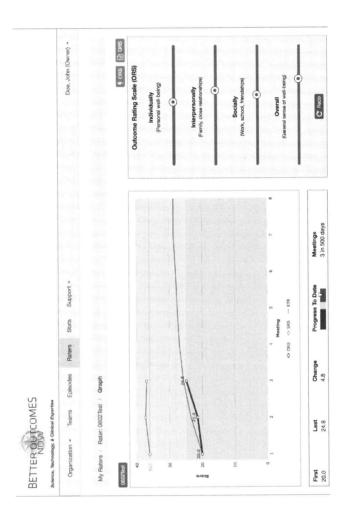

Figure 29.2 Better Outcomes Now (BON) graph displaying client's ORS scores (bottom line), ETR (middle line), and SRS scores (top line)

Strengths-based discussions. SBT supervisors regularly inquire about client strengths. This practice prompts a search for previously unrecognized client attributes and constructs new, more hopeful views of clients. Some openings for strengths-based discussions include:

- What do you like about this client?
- What are three primary strengths you see in this client?
- What resources does this client have to help with this situation?
- What might you say to this client that would prompt her to see herself as strong?
- When has this client not experienced this difficulty? How can those times give a clue to what s/he might try now?

Highlighting supervisee strengths. SBT supervisors pay attention to and comment on their supervisee's efforts and unique talents. This practice increases supervisees' sense of agency and engenders hope for their potential to help their clients and succeed professionally. SBT supervisors might say:

- I know it is not always easy for you to redirect what is happening, but you did! How did you do that?
- I really like how you remain hopeful in the face of this client's difficulties.
- How were you able to stay calm in this session with everything going on?

Focusing on supervisees' strengths acknowledges that each supervisee brings a unique set of life experiences, temperament, and preferences for engaging with others. SBT supervisors enhance client outcomes by helping supervisees flexibly adapt their unique personal attributes to match those of their clients.

Acting for social justice

Social justice involves:

promoting access and equity to ensure full participation of all people in the life of a society, particularly those who have been systematically excluded on the basis of race or ethnicity, gender, age, physical or mental disability, education, sexual orientation, socioeconomic status, or other characteristics of background or group membership.
(Lee & Hipolito-Delgado, 2007, p. xiv)

Social justice is uniquely relevant to the counseling profession because practitioners hold positions of power relative to their clients. By their very nature, helping relationships are unequal—helpers always have more power than those seeking help. Moreover, therapists tend to belong to dominant social groups with privileged access to educational and employment opportunities (American Psychological Association, 2015). A critical concern for mental health practitioners is how that privilege impacts counseling relationships, as well as client voice and choice.

Doing social justice

Three central principles of SBT closely align with social justice values:

1. all clients have strengths;
2. clients have a right to have their voices heard and respected;
3. clients' social contexts are essential to understanding and addressing their concerns.

The first two principles highlight clients' intrinsic strengths and worth, and the third illustrates the influence of socially defined categories on problem assessment and treatment. Together, they diminish client/therapist power differences and encourage collaborative partnerships. Client preferences are privileged over professional preferences. SBT clinicians *do* social justice when they put these principles into action. At the most immediate level, this involves giving a voice to clients, especially those who are marginalized. Socially just services put clients in the driver's seat. It is not unusual for therapists working in this way to hear clients remark "This is different!," "You listened to me!," or "I believe you really want to know what I think."

Strategies for doing socially just therapy have been detailed in this book and include the following:

- eliciting and incorporating client strengths throughout therapy;
- using client feedback to guide counseling decisions;
- co-developing and completing paperwork collaboratively with clients;
- avoiding pathological labels when possible (except when clients prefer them);
- using context assessments to portray client social resources and constraints;
- inviting clients to teach counselors about their customs, culture, and preferences, especially when there are significant differences between clients' and counselors' backgrounds;
- using everyday language (except when clients prefer more formal language);
- matching clients with counselors who speak their native language;
- engaging in outreach to clients and offering flexible meeting schedules when possible;
- involving neighborhoods and local communities in goal plans and change strategies, including alternative meeting locations and peer support.

Social justice counseling also involves various meeting protocols and strategies that include:

- incorporating client feedback forms into staff and supervisory meetings;
- including clients in agency staff meetings that involve their situation and goals;
- placing an empty chair in staff or supervision meetings to represent clients when they cannot be present;
- speaking up at staff or supervisory meetings to question the helpfulness of a diagnosis and recommend alternatives based on client descriptions.

Social justice advocacy

Giving voice to clients and integrating a focus on social context are powerful forms of social justice advocacy that help clinicians and clients re-conceptualize struggles as occurring within contexts unfavorable to clients in marginalized groups. This transformation helps clients reclaim their dignity and redefine themselves as survivors and heroes rather than succumbing to diagnostic descriptions. Counselors also can support clients' efforts to be their own advocates, especially in settings where power differences are salient (e.g., parent/school meetings or legal system or workplace concerns). Clients move from being passengers to being drivers of their lives.

Social justice advocacy also involves therapist actions beyond the therapy encounter that include efforts to change social structures that promote and sustain client distress. Scholars and activists have argued that not advocating for social change perpetuates problems frequently seen in psychotherapy (Vera & Speight, 2003). Counselors routinely bear witness to the impact of injustice when they listen to clients' stories—for example, raising a family on low wages or being victimized by racial or gender violence. A clinician's unwillingness to engage at a broader level disconnects clients' stories from their contexts and perpetuates individual explanations for understanding and resolving client difficulties. This diverts attention from social conditions that create or maintain client difficulties and undermines society's motivation to work for social change.

Acting to create a more just society may sound daunting. However, the goal is to work toward change in whatever capacity is feasible. Examples include:

- Create local networks of mental health service providers to collectively identify social barriers that impact their clients and create plans to address them.
- Write professional journal, magazine, or newsletter articles that address social justice concerns encountered in clinical practice.
- Write a letter or column to a local paper that calls attention to social inequities clients routinely face.
- Contact local and national representatives and politicians to advocate for changes in policies or areas that adversely impact clients.
- Join protests or other efforts that promote just social conditions for all persons.

There are countless other ways to advocate for social justice, and every person can decide what actions and level of involvement fit their talents, concerns, time, and energy. The key is to *do something*. The small and large efforts of many create change. Howard Zinn (2002) famously proclaimed: "You can't be neutral on a moving train." When we stand still, we help maintain business as usual. When clinicians support SBT principles and practices inside and outside the therapy room, they promote socially just mental health services and a more equitable society for all.

Appendix

Outcome Rating Scale (ORS), *Session Rating Scale* (SRS), *Child ORS* (CORS), and *Child SRS* (CSRS). Copyright 2000, 2002, 2003, and 2003 by B. L. Duncan and S. D. Miller. For examination only. Download free working copies in multiple languages at https://heartandsoulofchange.com

APPENDIX A

Outcome Rating Scale (ORS)

Name: _____ Age (Yrs): ____ Sex: M / F

Session # _____ Date: _____

Who is filling out this form? Please check one: Self _____ Other _____

If other, what is your relationship to this person? _____

Looking back over the last week, including today, help us understand how you have been feeling by rating how well you have been doing in the following areas of your life, where marks to the left represent low levels and marks to the right indicate high levels. *If you are filling out this form for another person, please fill out according to how you think he or she is doing.*

Individually

(Personal well-being)

|————————————————————————————————————|

Interpersonally

(Family, close relationships)

|————————————————————————————————————|

Socially

(Work, school, friendships)

|————————————————————————————————————|

Overall

(General sense of well-being)

|————————————————————————————————————|

The Heart and Soul of Change Project

www.heartandsoulofchange.com

© 2000, Scott D. Miller and Barry L. Duncan

APPENDIX A

Child Outcome Rating Scale (CORS)

Name: _____   Age (Yrs): ____   Sex: M / F
Session # ____   Date: _____
Who is filling out this form? Please check one: Child ____   Caretaker ____
If caretaker, what is your relationship to this child? _____

How are you doing? How are things going in your life? Please make a mark on the scale to let us know. The closer to the smiley face, the better things are. The closer to the frowny face, things are not so good. *If you are a caretaker filling out this form, please fill out according to how you think the child is doing.*

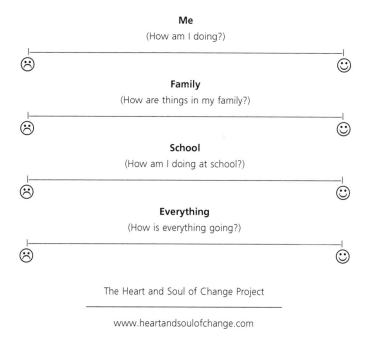

The Heart and Soul of Change Project

www.heartandsoulofchange.com

© 2003, Barry L. Duncan, Scott D. Miller, & Jacqueline A. Sparks

APPENDIX A

Session Rating Scale (SRS V.3.0)

Name: _____ Age (Yrs): ____
ID# _____ Sex: M / F
Session # ____ Date: _____

Please rate today's session by placing a mark on the line nearest to the description that best fits your experience.

Relationship

| I did not feel hear, understood, and respected. | |—————————————————| | I felt heard, understood, and respected. |

Goals and Topics

| We did not work on or talk about what I I wanted to work on and talk about. | |—————————————————| | We worked on and talked about what I wanted to work on and talk about. |

Approach or Method

| The therapist's approach is not a good fit for me. | |—————————————————| | The therapist's approach is a good fit for me. |

Overall

| There was something missing in the session today. | |—————————————————| | Overall, today's session was right for me. |

The Heart and Soul of Change Project

www.heartandsoulofchange.com

© 2002, Scott D. Miller, Barry L. Duncan, & Lynn Johnson

APPENDIX A

Child Session Rating Scale (CSRS)

Name: _____ Age (Yrs): _____
Sex: M / F
Session # _____ Date: _____

How was our time together today? Please put a mark on the lines below to let us know how you feel.

Listening

did not always listen to me. ☹ |————————————| ☺ listened to me.

How Important

What we did and talked about was not really that important to me. ☹ |————————————| ☺ What we did and talked about were important to me.

What We Did

I did not like what we did today. ☹ |————————————| ☺ I liked what we did today.

Overall

I wish we could do something different. ☹ |————————————| ☺ I hope we do the same kind of things next time.

The Heart and Soul of Change Project

www.heartandsoulofchange.com

© 2003, Barry L. Duncan, Scott D. Miller, Jacqueline A. Sparks

References

American Psychiatric Association (2013). *Diagnostic and statistical manual of mental disorders* (5th ed.). Washington, DC: Author.

American Psychological Association (2015). *Demographics of the U.S. psychology workforce: Findings from the American Community Survey*. Washington, DC: Author.

Andersen, T. (1992). Relationship, language and pre-understanding in the reflecting processes. *Australian and New Zealand Journal of Family Therapy*, *13*, 87–91. doi:10.1002/j.1467-8438.1992.tb00896.x

Anderson, H., & Gehart, D. (2007). *Collaborative therapy: Relationships and conversations that make a difference*. Abingdon, UK: Routledge Press.

Anderson, H., & Goolishian, H. (1988). Human systems as linguistic systems: Preliminary ideas about the implications for clinical theory. *Family Process*, *27*, 371–393.

Anderson, H., & Goolishian, H. (1992). The client is the expert: A not-knowing approach to therapy. In S. McNamee & K, Gergen (Eds.), *Therapy as social construction* (pp. 25–39). Newbury Park, CA: Sage.

Anker, M. G., Sparks, J. A., Duncan, B. L., Owen, J. J., & Stapnes, A. K. (2011). Footprints of couple therapy: Client reflections at follow-up. *Journal of Family Psychotherapy*, *22*, 22–45. doi:10.1080/08975353.2011.551098

APA Presidential Task Force on Evidence-Based Practice (2006). Evidence-based practice in psychology. *American Psychologist*, *61*, 271–285.

Baldwin, S. A., & Imel, Z. (2013). Therapist effects. In M. J. Lambert (Ed.), *Bergin and Garfield's handbook of psychotherapy and behavioral change* (6th ed., pp. 258–297). Hoboken, NJ: Wiley.

Balmforth, J. (2006). Clients' experiences of how perceived differences in social class between a counselor and client affect the therapeutic relationship. In G. Proctor, M. Cooper, P. Sanders, & B. Malcolm (Eds.), *Politicizing the person-centered approach: An agenda for social change* (pp. 215–224). Ross-on-Wye, UK: PCCS Books.

Barber, J. P., Muran, J. C., McCarthy, & Keefe, K. S., (2013). Research on dynamic therapies. In M. J. Lambert (Ed.), *Bergin and Garfield's handbook of psychotherapy and behavior change* (6th ed., pp. 443–494). Hoboken, NJ: Wiley.

Bateson, G., Jackson, D. D., Haley, J., & Weakland, J. (1956). Toward a theory of schizophrenia. *Behavioral Science*, *1*, 251–264. doi:10.1002/bs.3830010402

Berg, I. K. (1994). *Family based services: A solution-focused approach*. New York: W. W. Norton.

Berg, I. K., & de Shazer, S. (1993). Making numbers talk: Language in therapy. In S. Friedman (Ed.), *The new language of change: Constructive collaboration in psychotherapy*. New York: Guilford.

Beutler, L. E., Malik, M., Alimohamed, S., Harwood, T. M., Talebi, H., Noble, S., & Wong, E. (2004). Therapist variables. In M. J. Lambert (Ed.), *Bergin and Garfield's handbook of psychotherapy and behavior change* (5th ed., pp. 227–306). Hoboken, NJ: Wiley.

Bjorøy, A., Madigan, S., & Nylund, D. (2015). The practice of therapeutic letter writing in therapy. In B. Douglas, R. Woolfe, S. Strawbridge, E. Kasket, & V. Galbraith. (Eds.), *The handbook of counselling psychology* (4th ed., pp. 333–348). Thousand Oaks, CA: Sage.

Bohart, A., & Tallman, K. (2010). Clients: The neglected common factor in psychotherapy. In B. Duncan, S. Miller, B. Wampold, & M. Hubble (Eds.), *The heart and soul of change: Delivering what works in therapy* (2nd ed., pp. 83–111). Washington, DC: American Psychological Association. doi:10.1037/12075-003

Bohart, A., & Wade, A. G. (2013). The client in psychotherapy. In M. J. Lambert (Ed.), *Bergin and Garfield's handbook of psychotherapy and behavior change* (6th ed., pp. 219–257). Hoboken, NJ: Wiley.

Bordin, E. (1979). The generalizability of the psychoanalytic concept of the working alliance. *Psychotherapy*, *16*, 252–260.

Bourdieu, P. (1988) *Homo academicus*. Stanford, CA: Stanford University Press.

Bowlby, J. (1953). *Child care and the growth of love*. London: Penguin Books.

REFERENCES

Boyd-Franklin, N., Cleek, E. N., Wofsy, M., & Mundy, B. (2013). *Therapy in the real world: Effective treatments for challenging problems.* New York: Guilford Press.

Bronfenbrennner, U. (1979). *Ecology of human development: Experiments by nature and design.* Cambridge, MA: Harvard University Press.

Cantwell, P., & Holmes, S. (1994). Social construction: A paradigm shift for systemic therapy and training. *Australian and New Zealand Journal of Family Therapy, 15*(1), 17–26.

Caplan, P. J. (1995). *They say you're crazy: How the world's most powerful psychiatrists decide who's normal.* Jackson, MI: De Capo.

Carson, R. C. (1997). Costly compromises: A critique of The Diagnostic and Statistical Manual of Mental Disorders. In S. Fisher & R. P. Greenberg (Eds.), *From placebo to panacea: Putting psychiatric drugs to the test* (pp. 98–112). New York: Wiley.

Castonguay, L., Barkham, M., Lutz, W., & McAleavey, A. (2013). Practice-oriented research: Approaches and applications. In M. J. Lambert (Ed.), *Bergin and Garfield's handbook of psychotherapy and behavior change* (6th ed., pp. 85–133). Hoboken, NJ: Wiley.

Chang, D. F., & Yoon, P. (2011). Ethnic minority clients' perceptions of the significance of race in cross-racial therapy relationships. *Psychotherapy Research, 21,* 567–582.

Cooper, M. (2016). Core counselling methods for pluralistic practice. In M. Cooper & W. Dryden (Eds.), *The handbook of pluralistic counselling and psychotherapy* (pp. 80–91). London: Sage.

Cooper, M. & Dryden, W. (Eds.). (2016). *The handbook of pluralistic counselling and psychotherapy.* London: Sage.

Cooper, M., & McLeod, J. (2011). *Pluralistic counselling and psychotherapy.* London: Sage.

de Shazer, S. (1985). *Keys to solution in brief therapy.* New York: W. W. Norton.

de Shazer, S. (1988). *Clues: Investigating solutions in brief therapy.* New York: W. W. Norton.

de Shazer, S., Berg, I. K., Lipchik, E., Nunnally, E., Molnar, A., Gingerich, W., & Weiner-Davis, M. (1986). Brief therapy: Focused solution development. *Family Process, 25,* 207–222.

de Shazer, S., Dolan, Y., Korman, H., Trepper, T., McCollum, E., & Berg, I. K. (2007). *More than miracles: The state of the art of solution-focused brief therapy.* New York: Haworth Press.

Duncan, B. L. (2014). *On becoming a better therapist: Evidence based practice one client at a time* (2nd ed.). Washington, DC: American Psychological Association.

Duncan, B. L. (2017). Better Outcomes Now. Retrieved from https://betteroutcomesnow.com/#/.

Duncan, B. L., Miller, S. D., & Sparks, J. A. (2003a). Child Outcome Rating Scale. Retrieved from https://heartandsoulofchange.com.

Duncan, B. L., Miller, S. D., & Sparks, J. A. (2003b). Child Session Rating Scale. Retrieved from https://heartandsoulofchange.com.

Duncan, B., & Moynihan, D. (1994). Applying outcome research: Intentional utilization of the client's frame of reference. *Psychotherapy, 31*, 294–301.

Duncan, B. L., & Reese, R. J. (2015). The Partners for Change Outcome Management System (PCOMS): Revisiting the client's frame of reference. *Psychotherapy, 52*, 391–401.

Duncan, B. L., Solovey, A. D., & Rusk, G. S. (1992). *Changing the rules: A client-directed approach to therapy*. New York: Guilford Press.

Duncan, B., & Sparks, J. (2010). *Heroic clients, heroic agencies: Partners for change* (2nd ed.). Jensen Beach, FL: Author.

Dweck, C. S., & Master, A. (2008). Self-theories motivate self-regulated learning. In D. H. Schunk & B. J. Zimmerman (Eds.), *Motivation and self-regulated learning: Theory, research, and applications* (pp. 31–52). Mahwah, NJ: Erlbaum.

Egan, G. (2010). *The skilled helper: A problem-management and opportunity-development approach to helping* (9th ed.). Pacific Grove, CA: Brooks/Cole.

Elkins, D. N. (2016). *The human elements of psychotherapy*. Washington, DC: American Psychological Association.

Fiske, S. T., & Taylor, S. E. (2008). *Social cognition: From brains to culture*. New York: McGraw-Hill.

Foucault, M. (1972). *The archaeology of knowledge*. (A. M. Sheridan Smith, Trans.). New York: Pantheon.

Frances, A. (2012, October 31). DSM-5 field trials discredit the American Psychiatric Association (Web log post). Retrieved from www.huffingtonpost.com/allen-frances/dsm-5-field-trials-discre_b_2047621.html.

Frank J. D., & Frank, J. B. (1991). *Persuasion and healing: A comparative study of psychotherapy* (3rd ed.). Baltimore, MD: Johns Hopkins University Press.

Gassman, D., & Grawe, K. (2006). General change mechanisms: The relation between problem activation and resource activation in successful and unsuccessful therapeutic interactions. *Clinical Psychology and Psychotherapy, 13*, 1–11.

Gergen, K. (2009). *An invitation to social construction*. London: Sage.

Gergen, K. J. (1985). The social constructionist movement in modern psychology. *American Psychologist, 40*, 266–275.

Goodman, L. A., Liang, B., Helms, J. E., Latta, R. E., Sparks, E., & Weintraub, S. R. (2004). Training counseling psychologists as social justice agents: Feminist and multicultural principles in action. *The Counseling Psychologist, 32*, 793–836. doi:10.1177/0011000004268802

Greenberg, G. (2010, December). Inside the battle to define mental illness. *Wired*, 19. Retrieved from www.wired.com/magazine/2010/ff_dsmv.

Gurin, J. (1990). Remaking our lives. *American Health, 9*, 50–52.

Hatcher, R. L., & Barends, A. (1996). Patients' view of the alliance in psychotherapy: Exploratory factor analysis of three alliance measures. *Journal of Consulting and Clinical Psychology, 64*, 1326–1336.

Hill, M. (1998). *Feminist therapy as a political act*. New York: Routledge Press.

Hook, J. N., Davis, D. E., Owen, J., Worthington Jr., E. L., & Utsey, S. O. (2013). Cultural humility: Measuring openness to culturally diverse clients. Journal of *Counseling Psychology, 60*, 353–366. doi:10.1037/a0032595

Horvath, A. O., Del Re, A. C., Flückiger, C., & Symonds, D. (2011). Alliance in individual psychotherapy. *Psychotherapy, 48*, 9–16. doi:10.1037/a0022186

Howard, K. I., Moras, K., Brill, P. L., Martinovich, Z., & Lutz, W. (1996). Evaluation of psychotherapy: Efficacy, effectiveness, and patient progress. *American Psychologist, 51*, 1059–1064.

Hubble, M. A., Duncan, B. L., Miller, S. D, & Wampold. B. E. (2010). Introduction. In B. L. Duncan, S. D. Miller, B. E. Wampold, & M. A. Hubble (Eds.), *The heart and soul of change: Delivering what works in therapy* (2nd ed., pp. 23–46). Washington, DC: American Psychological Association.

Ivey, A. E., Ivey, M. B., & Zalaquett, C. P. (2014*). Intentional interviewing and counseling: Facilitating client development in a multicultural society* (8th ed.). Belmont, CA: Cengage Learning.

Kegel, A. F., & Flückiger, C. (2014). Predicting psychotherapy dropouts: A multilevel approach. *Clinical Psychology and Psychotherapy, 22*, 377–386. doi:10.1002/cpp.1899

Kendall, R., & Zablansky, A. (2003). Distinguishing between the validity and utility of psychiatric diagnoses. *American Journal of Psychiatry*, *160*, 4–12.

King, M. L. (1968). The role of the behavioral scientist in the civil rights movement. *Journal of Social Issues*, *XXIV*, 1–12.

Kirk, S. A., & Kutchins, H. (1992). *The selling of the DSM: The rhetoric of science in psychiatry*. New York: Aldine de Gruyter.

Kirsch, I. (2010). *The emperor's new drugs: Exploding the antidepressant myth*. New York: Basic Books.

Kupfer, D. J., First, M. B., Regier, D. A. (Eds.). (2002). *A research agenda for DSM-V*. Washington, DC: American Psychiatric Association.

Lambert, M. (2010). "Yes, it is time for clinicians to routinely monitor treatment outcome." In B. L. Duncan, S. D. Miller, B. E. Wampold, & M. A. Hubble (Eds.), *The heart and soul of change: Delivering what works in therapy* (2nd ed., pp. 239–266). Washington, DC: American Psychological Association.

Lambert, M. J. (2013). The efficacy and effectiveness of psychotherapy. In M. J. Lambert (Ed.), *Bergin and Garfield's handbook of psychotherapy and behavior change* (6th ed., pp. 169–218). Hoboken, NJ: Wiley.

Lambert, M. J., & Shimokawa, K. (2011). Collecting client feedback. *Psychotherapy*, *48*, 72–79. doi:10.1037/a0022238

Lee, C. C., & Hipolito-Delgado, C. P. (2007). Introduction: Counselors as agents of social justice. In C. C. Lee (Ed.), *Counseling for social justice* (2nd ed., pp. xiii–xxviii). Alexandria, VA: American Counseling Association.

Linssen, F., & Kerzbeck, U. (2002, September). Does solution-focused therapy work? Paper presented at the meeting of the European Brief Therapy Association, Cardiff, UK.

Maag, J. W. (2018). *Behavior management: From theoretical implications to practical applications* (3rd ed.). Boston, MA: Cengage Learning.

Madsen, W. C., & Gillespie, K. (2014). *Collaborative helping: A strengths framework for home-based services*. Hoboken, NJ: Wiley.

McGuire, W. J., & McGuire, C. V. (1996). Enhancing self-esteem by directed-thinking tasks: Cognitive and affective positivity asymmetries. *Journal of Personality and Social Psychology*, *70*, 1117–1125.

Miller, S. D., & Duncan, B. L. (2000). The Outcome Rating Scale. Retrieved from https://heartandsoulofchange.com.

Miller, S., Duncan, B., & Johnson, L. D. (2002). The Session Rating Scale. Retrieved from https://heartandsoulofchange.com.

Molden, D. C., & Dweck, C. S. (2006). Finding "meaning" in psychology: A lay theories approach to self-regulation, social perception, and social development. *American Psychologist, 61*, 192–203.

Murphy, J. J. (2015). *Solution-focused counseling in schools* (3rd ed.). Alexandria, VA: American Counseling Association.

Najavits, L. M., & Strupp, H. (1994). Differences in the effectiveness of psychodynamic therapists: A process-outcome study. *Psychotherapy, 31*, 114–123.

Norcross, J. (2010). The therapeutic relationship. In B. Duncan, S. Miller, B. Wampold, & M. Hubble (Eds.), *The heart and soul of change: Delivering what works* in therapy (2nd ed., pp. 113–142). Washington, DC: American Psychological Association.

Norcross, J., & Wampold, B. (2011). Evidence-based therapy relationships: Research conclusions and clinical practices. In J. C. Norcross (Ed.), *Psychotherapy relationships that work: Evidence-based responsiveness* (2nd ed., pp. 423–430). New York: Oxford University Press.

Orlinsky, D. E., Rønnestad, M. H., & Willutzki, U. (2004). Fifty years of process outcome research: Continuity and change. In M. J. Lambert (Ed.), *Bergin and Garfield's handbook of psychotherapy and behavior change* (5th ed., pp. 307–390). New York: Wiley.

Ozer, E. J., Best, S. R., Lipsey, T. L., & Weiss, D. S. (2008). Predictors of posttraumatic stress disorder and symptoms in adults: A meta-analysis. *Psychological Trauma: Theory, Research, Practice, and Policy, S*(1), 3–36. doi:10.1037/1942-9681.5.1.3

Pedersen, P. B. (2000). *Hidden messages in culture-centered counseling: A triad training model*. Thousand Oaks, CA: Sage.

Prilleltensky, I. (1999). Critical psychology foundations for the promotion of mental health. *Annual Review of Critical Psychology, 1*, 95–112.

Prochaska, J. O., Norcross, J. C., & DiClemente, C. C. (1994). *Changing for good*. New York: William Morrow.

Ramon, S., Healy, B., & Renouf, N. (2007). Recovery from mental illness as an emergent concept and practice in Australia and the UK. *International Journal of Social Psychiatry, 53*, 108–22.

Ricoeur, P. (1981). *Hermeneutics and the human sciences*. (J. Thompson (Ed.) & Trans). New York: Cambridge University Press.

Ridley, C. R. (2005). *Overcoming unintentional racism in counseling and therapy: A practitioner's guide to intentional intervention* (2nd ed.). Thousand Oaks, CA: Sage.

Rogers, C. R. (1951). *Client-centered therapy*. Boston, MA: Houghton Mifflin.

Saleebey, D. (2013). *The strengths perspective in social work practice* (6th ed.). New York: Pearson.

Seikkula, J., Aaltonen, J., Alakare, B., Haarakangas, K., Keränen, J., & Lehtinen, K. (2006). Five-year experience of first-episode nonaffective psychosis in open-dialogue approach: Treatment principles, follow-up outcomes, and two case studies. *Psychotherapy Research*, *16*, 214–228. doi:10.1080/10503300500268490

Seligman, M. P., Rashid, T., & Parks, A. C. (2006). Positive psychotherapy. *American Psychologist*, *61*, 774–788. doi:10.1037/0003-066X.61.8.774

Shapiro, J. P., Friedberg, R. D., & Bardenstein, K. K. (2006). *Child and adolescent therapy: Science and art*. New York: Wiley.

Sleek, S. (1998, December). Psychology's cultural competence, once "simplistic," now broadening. *Monitor on Psychology*, *29*, 1–27.

Snyder, C. R., Michael, S. T., & Cheavens, J. S. (1999). Hope as a psychotherapeutic foundation of common factors, placebos, and expectancies. In M. A. Hubble, B. L. Duncan, & S. D. Miller (Eds.), *The heart and soul of change: What works in therapy* (pp. 179–200). Washington, DC: American Psychological Association.

Sparks, J. A., & Duncan, B. L. (in press). Progress research in couple and family therapy. In J. L. Lebow, A. L. Chambers, & D. C. Breunlin (Eds.), *Encyclopedia of Couple and Family Therapy*. New York: Springer.

Sparks, J., & Duncan, B. (2018). The Partners for Change Outcome Management System: A both/and system for collaborative practice. *Family Process*. Early View https://onlinelibrary.wiley.com/toc/15455300/0/0.

Spiegel, A. (2005, January 3). The dictionary of disorder: How one man redefined psychiatric care. *The New Yorker*, 56–63.

Spinelli, E. (2015). *Practicing existential therapy: The relational world* (2nd ed.). London: Sage.

Sue, D. W. (2001). Multidimensional facets of cultural competence. *The Counseling Psychologist*, *29*, 790–821.

Sue, D. W., & Sue, D. (2016). *Counseling the culturally diverse: Theory and practice* (7th ed.). New York: Wiley.

Sue, S., & Zane, N. (2006). Ethnic minority populations have been neglected by evidence-based practices. In J. C. Norcross, L. E. Beutler, & R. F. Levant (Eds.), *Evidence-based practices in mental health: Debate*

REFERENCES

and dialogue on the fundamental questions (pp. 338–345). Washington, DC: American Psychological Association.

Tervalon, M. & Murray-García, J. (1998). Cultural humility versus cultural competence: A critical distinction in defining physician training outcomes in multicultural education. *Journal of Health Care for the Poor and Underserved*, *9*, 117–125. doi:10.1353/hpu.2010.0233

Vanheule, S., Desmet, M., Meganck, R., Inslegers, R., Willemsen, J., DeSchryver, M., Devisch, I. (2014). Reliability in psychiatric diagnosis: Old wine in new barrels. *Psychotherapy and Psychosomatics*, *83*, 313–314. doi:10.1159/000358809

Vera, E. M., & Speight, S. L. (2003). Multicultural competence, social justice, and counseling psychology: Expanding our roles. *The Counseling Psychologist*, *31*, 253–272. doi:10.1177/0011000003031003001

von Bertalanffy, L. (1968). *General systems theory: Foundations, development, applications*. New York: George Braziller.

Wampold, B. E. (2001). *The great psychotherapy debate: Models, methods, and findings*. Mahwah, NJ: Erlbaum.

Wampold, B. E., & Imel, Z. E. (2015). *The great psychotherapy debate: The evidence for what makes psychotherapy work* (2nd ed.). New York: Routledge Press.

Weiner, N. (1948). *Cybernetics, or control and communication in the animal and the machine*. New York: Wiley.

White, M. (2007). *Maps of narrative practice*. London: W. W. Norton.

White, M., & Epston, D. (1990). *Narrative means to therapeutic ends*. New York: W. W. Norton.

World Health Organization (2004). *The international statistical classification of diseases and related health problems: ICD-10*. Author: Geneva, Switzerland.

Zanarini, M. C., Frankenburg, F. R., Hennen, J., Reich, D. B., & Silk, K. (2006). Prediction of the ten year course of borderline personality disorder. *American Journal of Psychiatry*, *163*, 827–832.

Zinn, H. (2002). *You can't be neutral on a moving train*. Boston, MA: Beacon Press.

Index

alliance *see* therapeutic alliance
American Psychological Association 57
Anderson, H. 6
Anderson, T. 6
attachment theory 5

Bardenstein, K. 33
Barends, A. 26
Berg, I. 6
Better Outcomes Now (BON) 94, *95*, 122, *123*, 136, *137, 138*
between-session strategies 117–120
both-and perspective 61
Boyd-Franklin, N. 52
Bronfenbrenner, U. 46
"bump on a log" syndrome 19

centering client voice 135–136
challenges of SBT practice 61–64
"change ear" 98
Child Outcome Rating Scale (CORS) 122, 147
Child Session Rating Scale (CSRS) 122, 149
client-centered therapy 18

client-directed approach, 9–10, 17–20, 62, 70
client-directed, outcome informed (CDOI) practice 7
client expectancy *see* hope
client factors 9, 13, 21
client feedback *see* feedback
client involvement 9
client resiliency 15
client resources *see* resources
client theories of change 81–84
clients as consultants 114
clients as heroes of change 13–16
Clifton, D. 3
collaborative, client-directed dialogue 67–68
collaborative language systems 17
collaborative therapy 6
common factors of change 9–10, 13
compliments 75–77
confident collaboration 26
contextual perspective 53
Cooper, M. 7
counseling 4
cross-cultural exchange 67
cultural competency 50

cultural considerations in SBT 49–52
cultural humility 50
culture of one 67
cybernetic systems theory 5
cybernetics 45–46

de Shazer, S. 6
deficit-based practice 37
desired future 85–89
developing "next steps" 88
diagnosis and SBT 41–44
diagnostic reliability problems 41
Diagnostic Statistical Manual for Mental Disorders 41
diagnostic validity problems 41
discourse theory 38
Duncan B. 7, 9, 17, 81
Dweck, C. 29

ecological systems theory 46
environmental assessment 127
Epston, D. 6, 111
Erickson, M. 3
exceptions to the problem: 6, 92, 99; building on 105–109
expected treatment response 136–137
externalizing: conversations 111–114; metaphors 113; the problem 6

family therapy 5
feedback: in CDOI practice 7; collecting from clients 57–59, 121–125; systematic client feedback (PCOMS) 10–11, 54, 57, 99, 121, 136
feminist-influenced therapies 7
Flückiger, C. 26

Frances, A. 42
Frank, J (Jerome) 29
Frank, J (Julia) 29
Friedberg, R. 33
future-focused conversations 77–78

Gassman, D. 35
general systems theory 45
gentle encouragement 118–119
Gergen, K. 38
goals: agreement on 26; positive 88; questions 82; setting 26; small 88; specific 88
Goolishian, H. 6
Grawe, K. 35

Hatcher, R. 26
Heart and Soul of Change Project 58
History of SBT 3–8
hope 29–31; *see also* instilling hope

instilling hope: offering compliments 75–77; facilitating future-focused conversations 77–79

Kegel, A. 26
King, M. 55

language: in SBT 37–39; power of 87; in SBT Site Assessment Grid 128
letters 117–118
listening for change 97–100
lists 120

McLeod J. 7
medical: assumption 42; formula of diagnosing problems and

INDEX

prescribing treatments 10; jargon 130
medical model 10
mental health discourse 37–39
minimal encouragers 71–72
misunderstandings of "strengths-based" 10–11
Moynihan, D. 17

narratives: "counter-narratives" 112; social and cultural 34 *see also* stories
narrative therapy 6, 18, 111, 135
National Registry of Evidence Based Programs and Practices (NREBP) 57

observation tasks 119–120
Outcome Questionnaire-45.2 System (OQ) 57–58
Outcome Rating Scale (ORS) 58, 85, 94, *95,* 99, 121–122, 136, 146

paperwork 130; in SBT Site Assessment Grid 128
Partners for Change Outcome Management System (PCOMS) 18, 58–59, 121–125; as a dialogical tool 122–125
Pedersen, P. 52
Persuasion and Healing 29
placebo effect 29
pluralistic therapy 7
positive psychology 4
post-graduate training 134–135
postmodern therapies 5–7
preferred stories 111 *see also* stories
presupposition 78

Prilleltensky, I. 55
problem activation 23
problem-focused assessment 93
psychology 4

questions 101–104; about desired future 87; approach 83; change 82–83; coping 101–102; exception-seeking 106; externalizing 112; goal 82; in supervision 136; person-influence 113; problem-focused 93; problem-influence 112; relative influence 112; resilience 101–102; resource-focused 93; solution 83

recovery movement 8
social supports: as client factor 9; recruiting 114
resource activation 23
resources: as a client factor 9; assessment of 93; identifying and applying 52; incorporation of 94; recruiting client 91–94
respectful curiosity 67–70
Reynolds, B. 4
Rogers, C. 18, 26

SBT Site Assessment Grid *128*
self-efficacy 29
Session Rating Scale (SRS) 58, 138, 122, 148
Shapiro, J. 33
social action 55
social constructionism 33–35, 38
social justice: acting for 141–144; and SBT 53–56

163

social-linguistic factors 34
social work 4
solution-focused therapy 6, 18, 105; assumptions of 98
Spitzer, R. 41
stories: co-creating new 111–115; of failure and deficiency; preferred 111; strengths-based 44
strength identification 62
strengths-based therapy procedures 129–130
Substance Abuse and Mental Health Administration (SAMHSA) 57
supervision *see* training in SBT
systematic client feedback *see* feedback
systemic theory 45; implications for SBT 46–47; limitations 47–48

therapeutic alliance 25–27; monitoring 26–27; repair 26–27; client-therapist 10, 14, 25
therapist effects 21; maximizing 21–23
training in SBT: graduate 133–134; post-graduate 134–135; supervision 135–139
transtheoretical quality of SBT 9–11

validation: of clients 71–74; direct 71–72; indirect 71–72
value-added quality of SBT 9–11
von Bertalanffy, L. 45

Weiner, N. 45
White, M. 6, 111, 115
work environments: assessing 127–129; creating strengths-based 127–131